green earth guide

traveling naturally in

FRANCE

green earth guide

traveling naturally in
FRANCE

North Atlantic Books
Berkeley, California

Published by
North Atlantic Books
P.O. Box 12327
Berkeley, California 94712

Cover photo of herboristerie and interior photos by Dorian Yates
Cover photo of vegetables © iStockphoto.com/Click
Cover photo of lavender fields © iStockphoto.com/Marc Lobjoy
Cover and book design by Claudia Smelser
Printed in the United States of America

Green Earth Guide: Traveling Naturally in France is sponsored by the Society for the Study of Native Arts and Sciences, a nonprofit educational corporation whose goals are to develop an educational and cross-cultural perspective linking various scientific, social, and artistic fields; to nurture a holistic view of arts, sciences, humanities, and healing; and to publish and distribute literature on the relationship of mind, body, and nature.

North Atlantic Books' publications are available through most bookstores. For further information, visit our Web site at www.northatlanticbooks.com or call 800-733-3000.

LIBRARY OF CONGRESS CATALOGING-IN-PUBLICATION DATA

Yates, Dorian.
  Green Earth guide : traveling naturally in France / Dorian Yates. —1st ed.
    p. cm.
  ISBN 978-1-55643-806-6
  1. France—Guidebooks. 2. Environmental responsibility—France.
  3. Green movement—France. 4. Sustainable living—France.
  5. Ecotourism—France. I. Title.
  GE199.F8Y384 2009

  914.404'84—dc22   2009001901

1 2 3 4 5 6 7 8 9 United 14 13 12 11 10 09

To Kit, Cary, Nort, Chessie, and Art
To Joanne and Nell, angels in my dark days
And to Phil, who is always alive in my heart

acknowledgments

Preparing my thank you list makes me more sympathetic to the oft-lampooned Academy Award speeches that thank everyone under the sun. Obviously, time and space do not allow for this, but I now understand the temptation. Life is so full of serendipitous exchanges and meetings, and it feels as if everyone who has ever crossed my path has contributed to this book in one way or another—to them I give my sincerest thanks. A few people need special acknowledgment, and they are the folks at North Atlantic Books, who have been a delight to work with; my beloved husband and children, who supported and encouraged me through it all, and who endure all my craziness; my dear Putney friends in Europe—Arnold, Carlta, and Doina, and their families—who housed and fed me, and offered warmth, and enthusiasm; my sister-like friends, Leigh Chesnut and Lis Macaulay, who helped with ideas, editing, and encouragement; Mary Louise Pierson, for laughter and support; Red, who has helped more than he could know; and my mother, who named me Dorian, without which none of this might have happened.

table of contents

how to use this book

The *Green Earth Guides* are designed to help travelers find ethical and green options easily. The goal is to make your traveling experience greener for you and the environment. This guide is organized into four chapters. The first chapter explores the importance of considering the environment in your consumer and travel choices. The second chapter is about ecotravel in particular and discusses Europe-wide green travel information. The third chapter is the heart of the book, and it provides country-specific information, including listings of most things green and alternative in France. The final section is brief, and lists select foreign words to help you travel naturally, as well as resources to help you find updates and additional information about *Green Earth Guides* and traveling naturally.

To get you in the spirit of traveling naturally in France, I have chosen to include French terms in a number of the sections. The French word for organic is *biologique,* or *bio* for short, and I have used *bio* (pronounced "beeo") in many places throughout the book. *Bio* combined with any word indicates an organic product: in French, organic wine is *bio vin,* an organic cosmetic is *cosmétique bio,* and an organic market is *marché biologique* (pronounced "marchay beeola-jeek"). Getting comfortable and familiar with these terms will make traveling naturally in France a good deal easier.

In order to provide you with the maximum amount of information available, I have provided addresses for many Web sites. However, some of the Web sites listed are only available in French. Where this is the case, I have tried to illustrate the easiest way to reach the pertinent information. Some Web sites are available in both French and

Some helpful words to know while using a French-language Web site:

magasin = store

trouver notre magasins = find our stores

points de vente = points of sale or retail outlets

liens = links

découvrir = discover

hébergement = accommodation

télécharger = download

accueil = home page

l'alimentation = food

l'alimentation biologique = organic food

produits = products

English. In these cases, the English version is often available by finding and clicking on a small British flag, usually found in the upper right or left corner of the Web page. Look carefully, however, as sometimes the flag can be found at the bottom of the page. See **Web Site Navigation Tips** for useful French words.

THE FINE PRINT

Great care and attention have gone into the preparation of this guidebook, but prices change, places move or close, schedules get revised. Please understand that these alterations are beyond our control, and that neither the author nor North Atlantic Books is liable for any loss, inconvenience, or injury. All health information and resources listed in the *Green Earth Guide* are for educational purposes only. Please use the information responsibly.

The degree to which ecological principles are incorporated varies greatly between accommodations. Some will cover many or all the criteria listed below, others will integrate only one or some of them.

- Serve organic and local food
- Situated on land managed by organic methods
- Employ renewable energy for electricity and/or heating
- Employ water and energy conservation methods and energy-efficient systems
- Use natural-fiber bedding and linens
- Use natural and renewable building materials in construction and furnishing
- Renovated an old building (as a form of recycling)
- Use environmentally friendly cleaning products
- Accessible by public transportation and/or near or on biking/hiking routes
- Use recycled products, such as toilet paper
- Practice a laundry-reduction program
- Provide on-site recycling
- Maintain a no-smoking facility
- Make use of an existing facility, such as a home or farm, as a bed-and-breakfast, and/or efficiently use space, such as multi-bed rooms in hostels

Traveling Naturally Whys and Wherefores

All the sites and businesses are listed at my discretion and pleasure, based on my experience of over thirty years working on environmental issues and with ecoconscious businesses, coupled with my personal passion for all things natural. In order to keep the guide light and small enough for easy traveling, I have chosen to concentrate on certain regions, providing more detail for some and Web-based search options for others, in order to maximize the accessibility of useful information. Whichever way you make use of these resources, I hope this *Green Earth Guide* makes your travels healthier and greener.

Accommodation choices in the *Green Earth Guides* include hostels, guesthouses, home exchanges, and camping. These tend to be low-impact, small-scale, local enterprises with concern for the environment. Recycling systems are usually available, bedding is not changed every day, and small plastic bottles of synthetically perfumed toiletries are not available for you to use, take home, or throw away. These accommodation choices usually offer greater cultural experiences, and are cozier and more interesting than chain hotels. Some of the super-green eco-accommodations use solar or wind power and serve organic food (see *Green Earth Guide* Accommodations sidebar).

Food choices include large and small health food stores, organic and fair-trade labels, gluten-free brands, and local farm stands. By choosing organic and local foods you support a cleaner, more just and sustainable environment. Organic food has been found to have higher nutrients than conventionally grown food, which means you will be taking better care of yourself, too.

Recreation information focuses on outdoor activities, especially hiking and biking, that have no or low environmental impact. Meditation and yoga facilities are included, as well as locations of hot mineral baths. Where applicable, outdoor film and theater venues are listed.

Due to their much smaller environmental footprint, complementary and alternative medicine choices are considered green options. Natural plant-based remedies have been used for millennia without the environmental degradation caused by pharmaceutical drugs. Many researchers, including those in Germany, Switzerland, Italy, Canada, and the United States, have found dozens of drugs in our water and soil. Water contaminants include acetaminophen, caffeine, anti-epileptics, antibiotics, antidepressants, beta-blockers and lipid regulators, chemotherapy drugs, and anti-microbials. The antidepressant Prozac has even been discovered in earthworms. Research results suggest that mixtures of drugs can affect human health at a cellular level and potentially affect the health of aquatic life. The global environmental consequences may include bacterial resistance to medications, endocrine (hormone) disruption in fish, humans, and other animals, and generally lower immune resistance and response in humans.

Alternative health care has a long history in Europe, and is not considered "alternative" in many countries. Europe is replete with health practitioners, including massage therapists, natural doctors, and traditional Chinese medical doctors. Spas and clinics are plentiful, and natural remedies are often sold alongside pharmaceutical medicines in drugstores. There are many brands of high-quality personal care products, such as shampoos, soaps, and cosmetics, which are made with natural and organic ingredients.

Shopping information focuses on where to purchase natural, untreated, organic items, and includes secondhand stores, fair-trade products, and local specialties. Thrift or secondhand stores are wonderful places to shop. Full of clothes, books, art, furniture, kitchen gadgets and more, they are a treasure trove for travelers interested in recycling and reusing items. These shopping choices are respectful of the environment, the artisans, and the local economy. When purchasing secondhand goods, you also help to reduce the global load of consumer products.

Ecobusinesses and other places of interest are chosen based on their intrinsically natural and ecological characteristics, as well as on their historical significance and natural beauty. Listings include organic farms and vineyards, wind farms, World Heritage environmental areas, bird and wildflower information, sacred and mystical sites, and ecotourism highlights.

It is rewarding to work with people in a foreign country towards a common goal, and such work greatly deepens your bond with a place and its citizens. It is for these reasons I have included a small section on volunteer tourism.

one **whole view**

The Green Earth Guide: Traveling Naturally in France is designed for any and all travelers inclined to make green choices. It is not about choosing the most enticing ecotour. It is about extending your lifestyle choices and intentions to your world of travel. By choosing green options, you help support local economies, local ecologies, and the greater environment, treading a little more lightly on the earth.

The Environmental Footprint of Our Lives

Whether we like it or not, we all add to the ever-increasing environmental degradation that plagues our planet. The choices and decisions we make, from crackers to car purchases, impact the degree of our contribution—the veritable size of our personal environmental footprint.

Global warming, caused by various chemical and environmental interactions that heat the atmosphere, is largely due to carbon dioxide emissions. For millennia, naturally occurring carbon has played a role in keeping the earth appropriately insulated from frigid outer space. In the last 150 years, humans have been releasing growing volumes of carbon into the atmosphere from coal, oil and other sources, which disrupts the carbon balance, allowing the earth's atmosphere to become increasingly warmer.

Americans currently leave the largest environmental footprint, with an average annual carbon dioxide emission of sixty thousand pounds per person. Europeans produce about half that amount per person, and the Japanese produce less than half —they are acknowledged as the most energy-efficient of all developed countries. By contrast, the carbon emission on the part of the average Bangladeshi is less than six hundred pounds—that's 1 percent of the average American footprint.

If you travel by air, you can quickly add to your carbon footprint. One round-trip flight between the United States and Europe can add between two to four tons of carbon emissions. Calculations depend on exact flight distance and class of travel. Economy seats, while uncomfortable, are calculated at a lower per-person emission—a small consolation for little or no legroom. One transatlantic flight generates more carbon than twenty Bangladeshi people will produce in a year.*

Whether we realize it or not, everything we do and every choice we make has political and far-reaching effects. The more conscious and intentional we can be about how we live our lives, the greater the effect on the whole, and the smaller the footprint we leave. Many people understand this, and many people want to do the right thing for themselves and the world. This is why the green movement has been driven by consumer demand, not by corporate business interests.

Small footprints come in many sizes. We can make choices and decisions about little things and big things. We can follow one eco-option, or many. The more we do, the more we contribute to the ripple effect. As the ripple becomes a wave—a wave of increasingly environmentally sound ways to live and be on Earth—the smaller our footprints become.

As consumers, individual and collective purchasing power is enormous. Our footprints become smaller by supporting and frequenting businesses involved with organic and whole foods, efficient and renewable energy, recycling, natural and untreated products, natural health care and local enterprises. This breeds diversity, healthy land, water and air, and vital local economies—all healthier for you and the world.

Flying Green: How to Protect the Climate & Travel Responsibly, Tufts Climate Initiative & Stockholm Environment Institute; www.tufts.edu/tie/tci/carbonoffsets/TCI-offset-handout.htm.

It is critically important to offset the carbon footprints from air travel. The concept behind carbon-offset programs is to make reparations for emissions that we generate daily, as well as occasionally, like air travel. This usually involves paying for offsets through various organizations in the form of a donation or purchase.

Recently there has been an explosion of organizations and businesses that offer programs to offset carbon emissions. Some of these organizations invest in renewable and energy efficiency programs, some in reforestation initiatives. Whether or not you contribute to these efforts while at home, it can be beneficial to do so when you are traveling by plane since calculations show that one transatlantic round-trip flight generates over one to four tons of carbon dioxide per person. You can donate to any of the organizations listed below, or contribute to one of your favorite environmental groups.

Carbon-Offset Programs

Carbon Fund puts donations towards efficiency and renewable energy, as well as reforestation programs. Carbon Fund estimates that an individual generates about twenty-three tons of carbon per year, which they calculate at an annual donation for their offset programs of $99 for an individual or $326 for a family. The Carbon Fund Web site offers details about offset programs, climate change, and more. For more information, go to www.carbonfund.org.

CNDo Scotland works with the National Trust of Scotland to offset carbon emissions by focusing on native peat restoration projects to conserve, restore, and expand peat moorlands, a primary "sink" for carbon. For more information, go to www.cndoscotland.com/carbon-conservation.

Sustainable Travel International offers information for travelers about ecotravel tours and their carbon-offset program, Green Class, which promotes renewable and energy-efficient technologies in developing countries. They calculate one round-trip flight from Boston to Zurich at 2.28 tons of carbon generated per person with an offset donation cost of $34.77. For more information, go to www.sustainabletravelinternational.org.

Conservation International works around the world conserving biodiversity through rainforest preservation, conservation, and reforestation programs. Their carbon calculator finds that an average individual generates twenty-four tons of carbon a year, and their annual donation suggestion to offset that quantity is $240. For an average American driver they suggest $50 annually to offset the emission effects. For more information, go to www.conservation.org.

Focusing particularly on Native American land, NativeEnergy is focused on developing and supporting renewable energy projects, which include the first large-scale wind farm in South Dakota owned and operated by Native Americans, as well as three wind projects in Alaskan native villages where NativeEnergy is working to decrease the reliance on diesel-powered electricity. For more information, go to www.nativeenergy.com.

Global Warming and the Environment

In addition to carbon-offset programs, there are numerous organizations working on global warming and other environmental issues. The groups listed below offer educational and action resources.

The Natural Resources Defense Council (NRDC) works on a wide range of environmental issues, from air and water quality to wildlife protection, to sustainable energy and waste management. They are known for their staff of excellent consumer advocates and legal experts. For more information, go to NRDC's global warming information page at www.nrdc.org/globalwarming/default.asp.

The Stop Global Warming Campaign provides information about the dangers of global warming and tools to help you reduce your personal carbon emissions. They run a virtual march that can be accessed on their Web site at www.stopglobalwarming.org.

Personal carbon calculators can be found at Earth Future, which offers a list of organizations and Web sites from around the world that provide calculation services. For more information, go to www.earthfuture.com/climate/calculators.

Ben & Jerry's Ice Cream and the Dave Matthews Band have joined forces for the Lick Global Warming Campaign. While anyone can participate, the campaign is geared towards children. Young and old can visit the site at www.lickglobalwarming.org/learn.cfm.

Background information on the movie *An Inconvenient Truth* is available at www.climatecrisis.net/thescience.

Climate Counts, a campaign organized by Stonyfield Organic Yogurt, is focused on consumer and corporate responsibility. The site offers company scorecards so you can view what actions businesses are taking to reduce their environmental footprint. You will also find a downloadable, pocket shopping guide to help you make the best ecochoices. Visit Climate Counts at www.climatecounts.org.

The International Panel on Climate Change, part of the United Nations Environmental Program, can be found at www.ipcc.ch.

two go lightly

The Mind-set of Traveling Naturally and Lightly

1. Be Where You Are: Stay connected to the local environment by taking the time to see, feel, and appreciate where you are.
2. Tread Lightly: Ecofriendly, low-impact choices are good for nature, good for you, good for the environment, and good for the world.

There is a state of mind that seeks out the other side of life—the vast network and virtual underground of organic and fresh foods, natural fibers, natural colors and scents, local farms and working land. This mind-set sees the beauty of humans working with the earth and with technologies that harness the bounty of the natural world, not trying to conquer, overpower, and destroy it. This mind-set notices gardens tucked into the crevices of life, between rail tracks and otherwise underutilized plots of land. This mind-set marvels at the beauty of a window box full of flowers, the colors of the buildings, the history and continuity of cultures. This mind-set honors our human differences and similarities.

Keep this viewpoint in mind as you make use of the information and resources included in this book, and as you make your own discoveries. Remember that cultural history often informs daily habits. Most European countries, dealing with a lack of space and a history of war, have daily routines that many Americans consider trends or movements. For instance, a small country like Switzerland (twice the size of Massachusetts) has had no choice but to work with what they have, minimizing pollution and waste and maximizing beauty and cleanliness. For example, purchases like laundry detergent, rubbing alcohol, and hydrogen peroxide often come in refillable containers that you can replenish at the local drugstore or grocery store.

So, get into the groove! Bring your bags or baskets to the markets. Be ready to refill bottles, and to recycle when you can't refill. And get ready to enjoy the more inherently green infrastructure of many European destinations.

Before You Go
HEALTH

Travelers to Europe have many alternative remedies and treatments readily available. Some very helpful tips for general travel, and extensive homeopathic information for traveling where serious illness is more endemic, can be found in *The World Travellers' Manual of Homeopathy*, by Dr. Colin B. Lessell.

For the traveler inclined to alternative and natural health care, it is a good idea to prepare your own travel health care kit. Essentials include lavender essential oil (for relaxation, to conceal bad smells, and as a mild antiseptic); Emergen-C vitamin C individual packets (for sickness prevention and for rehydration and energy during air travel); *Andrographis paniculata* tablets (for sickness prevention and shortening sickness duration); magnesium (for muscle cramps and to prevent traveler constipation); arnica gel (for sore muscles try Traumeel, made by the HEEL company in Germany and sold worldwide).

Make sure any liquids and gels come in small container sizes (three ounces or less) if you are carrying them on the airplane.

If you are planning a trip involving spa or clinic reservations, make sure to schedule ahead, as many appointments are booked out for three months or longer.

MONEY

Planning ahead can save you money when you travel. Check with your existing bank to see if the debit/credit card on your account charges foreign transaction fees (most do). If they do not, you are in

If you are gluten sensitive or allergic, but do not have celiac disease, you may want to add Glutenzyme capsules to your natural health care travel kit. The enzymes can be helpful when traveling, especially when you find yourself surrounded by the plentiful wheat products often served as part of your inclusive accommodation breakfast and at numerous local bakeries. Pharmax makes a similar product for people who are lactose intolerant called Dairy-Ease. For more information, go to Pharmax Nutriceutical and Biophysical Systems www.pharmaxllc.com.

luck! Use that card for all or most of your overseas expenses—both ATM withdrawals and credit transactions. You will save significant money this way. There are usually separate daily security limits for cash withdrawal and credit transactions. If your current card does charge a fee for each foreign transaction, shop around and see if any other local banks offer a card without those charges. Most major credit card companies do charge between 1 and 9 percent on each transaction, and between 1 and 3 percent on debit cards. You can find helpful card fee comparison charts using the "Resources" link at the Travel Finances Web site. For more information, go to www.travelfinances.com.

ECOTRAVEL PREPARATION

Be prepared for your *Green Earth Guide* travel. Pack a few lightweight but sturdy reusable shopping bags, as you will need these for shopping of any kind. You may want to practice the language of your destination. The BBC Languages Web site offers free courses in French, Italian, Spanish, German, and other languages. For more information, go to www.bbc.co.uk/languages.

The Essentials List

1. Medium-size, lightweight daypack.

2. Up to four canvas or other reusable shopping-size bags, not too heavy, with good handles.

3. Extremely comfortable long-distance walking shoes and Smart Wool™ socks.

4. Natural health care kit (details listed above at **Before You Go**).

5. Natural hand sanitizers with essential oils, like Tea Tree oil and lavender, rather than antibacterial chemicals. These come available as wipes in individual foil packs (Desert Essence brand) or in small bottles (EO Organic Lavender Hand Sanitizer). The wipes are great to carry on the airplane, as they meet the criteria for allowable items. You can pack the bottle in your checked luggage.

6. Reusable water bottle.

7. A small language guide or dictionary.

8. Appropriate electrical adapters.

9. Mini reading light or flashlight.

10. Hostel member card (if you are planning to stay at hostels).

For the ultimate green travel, you can buy a backpack with solar panels that recharge your cell phone and digital audio player. Voltaic solar bags come in five different sizes and four colors, and they are made from recycled soda bottles. Prices range from $199 to $249. The most expensive option is the Generator at $599, and it produces enough power to charge a laptop. You can purchase the bags online or at one of their many stores around the world. For more information, go to www.voltaicsystems.com.

At Earth Tech Products you can find many solar bags, including Voltaic. Earth Tech offers a solar camera bag, a solar bicycle trunk bag, and a solar tackle bag. Prices range from $113 to $239. For more information, go to www.earthtechproducts.com/solar-backpacks.html. Juice Bags, a solar bag from Reware, comes in several convenient, hip styles. PowerPockets, also available from Reware, are solar panel strips that can be used to charge your electronics. They fold up and are easy to carry in a bag or a large pocket. Prices start at $150 for the PowerPockets and go up to $300 for some of the Juice Bags. For more information, go to www.rewarestore.com.

DRY-CLEANING AND LAUNDRY

Dry-cleaning involves a chemical called perchloroethylene, referred to as "perc," which has been found to adversely affect the nervous

Clothes dryers are uncommon in Europe, even in private homes, so bring clothes that dry quickly naturally. Many youth hostels do have washers and dryers available for a fee. Public laundromats, called *laveries automatique*, are common in France.

system, liver, and kidneys. It is considered a possible carcinogen. Perchloroethylene poses risks not only to human and animal health, but also to air and water quality. California recently passed a law to phase out all perc-based dry-cleaning systems by 2023.

While there are some alternatives to traditional dry-cleaning that are being touted as green—wet-cleaning, and systems using silicone or carbon dioxide–based solvents—there are questionable aspects to their processing. Since ecological dry-cleaning options are not yet readily available, the ecotraveler is best advised to avoid packing dry-clean-only garments.

Europe-wide Information and Resources
TRANSPORTATION

Car Rentals
For environmental reasons this book is focused on public transportation, as well as travel by foot and by bicycle. For destinations or schedules that require a car, take heart. While currently there are no ecocar rentals in Europe, most cars are ecofriendly by default. In Europe, economy and standard class cars usually get thirty to fifty miles to the gallon, often using no-fume diesel and efficient engines. This is due not only to the long standing higher fuel prices in Europe, but also to the fact that older, smaller roads, built long before cars were invented, require smaller cars. These efficient cars are available at both local rental companies and global car rental companies, such as Avis, Hertz, and others.

Walking
The Web site Walk On Web—in English, French, German, and Dutch—has digital sources of various hiking and walking routes

through many European countries and includes a free walk planner. You can choose the length of walk, its intensity, its proximity to public transport, and more. The site is still under development, so not all regions are represented, but it is very helpful for those that are. For more information, go to www.walkonweb.org.

The European Ramblers' Association has a terrific Web site—in English, French, and German—and includes illustrations of the eleven long-distance walking paths that cross Europe. For more information, go to www.era-ewv-ferp.com.

National Geographic "Walks of a Lifetime" podcasts are fun, free, and informative. Each one is about fifteen to twenty minutes long. The program includes locations in Amsterdam, Barcelona, Berlin, London, Paris, Rome, Venice, and Vienna. Download the podcasts from www.nationalgeographic.com/podcasts/walks.html.

Rail Travel

A word to the ecowise: Traveling by train or bus generates three to seven times fewer emissions than plane travel.

For schedules, prices, itinerary planning, and in-country rail passes, see the French rail service Web site listed under Public Transportation in the *Traveling Naturally in France* chapter.

For multi-country rail passes it is best to comparison shop online at several European rail pass sites, although many of them really are selling the same passes at similar prices. For instance, the Europe Global pass is only available in first class, and the cost remains pretty consistent no matter which site you peruse: $1279 at www.railpass.com, $1281 at www.raileurope.com, or $1279 at www.eurail.com. The Eurail site offers a special second-class pass that costs $835 for travelers under 25. (Prices are accurate at the time of writing. Please check the Web sites for current pricing.)

Before you buy a rail pass, check out the differences between a rail pass and point-to-point fares at www.ricksteves.com/rail/comparetickets.htm. The Rick Steves' site has lots of helpful information, and reminds travelers that a rail pass is not always the most affordable solution for your travel plans. The site also offers a handy, printable worksheet to organize your travel plans and chart the best deals. It also includes a map with approximate fares between European cities.

Rick Steves' Guide to Eurail Passes, a downloadable PDF guide, is full of useful information to help you sort through the fine print. If you are purchasing a rail pass you should know that the Eurostar train between London and the continent does not honor the pass. However, if you book in advance there are sometimes a limited number of special reduced fare seats for rail pass holders. For more information about Eurostar options, go to www.eurostar.com or www.raileurope.com.

For destinations not accessible by train, the Bus Station Web site has links to many bus Web sites all over the world, and it is searchable by continent and country. For more information, go to www.busstation.net.

COMMUNICATION AND PHONE CALLS

In the burgeoning world of the Internet, printed phone books have become increasingly hard to find. If you need to look up a business or friend, see www.europe.org/yellowpages.html for a list of European countries and their respective yellow pages.

Inexpensive calling cards can be purchased in most countries and are recommended. If you wish to purchase in advance, cards are available online. With any calling card, make certain to check the per-minute rate, the connection fee (a flat rate charge for connecting the call), the billing increment (a charge per minute or multiple minutes), and look to see if there is pay phone surcharge fee. Understanding all the card fees will help you avoid any surprise charges. Also, find out if the card is "rechargeable" or if you need to purchase a new one each time you run out of minutes. For more information, go to www.callingcards.com.

Hostelling International offers international calling cards as part of their membership benefits (see contact information under **Accommodations**). Remember to compare all calling card fees and rates.

Voice-over-Internet Protocol (VoIP) programs are worth considering. Skype is a free download system that allows you to talk computer to computer. Like many cell phone plans, these calls are free if made from one Skype user to another Skype user. If you are calling a non-Skype user, however, there are charges. For Skype calls to work, your computer will need a microphone and some sort of high-speed Internet access. If your computer has a camera, you can also enjoy video calls. You can see friends and family at home, and they get a chance to see you, which is a great option while traveling. For more information, go to www.skype.com.

To locate Wi-Fi spots go to www.wifinder.com and search by country.

ACCOMMODATIONS

For hostel information, Hostelling International (HI) runs the most comprehensive Web site at www.hihostels.com. From there you can access hostel information all over the world. To become a member, visit the U.S. site at www.hiusa.org. You will need a membership to stay at many of the hostels. Annual membership is $28 and children under 18 are free.

A good source for non-HI hostels and budget hotels can be found at www.hostelscentral.com. Check this site for options in locations where Hostelling International does not have hostels.

When the weather is amenable, camping is an inexpensive and environmentally friendly option, but make sure you pitch your tent at a designated campground. Camping in unofficial campsites is prohibited in most European countries. See the country-specific information for campground listings.

Green Travel: The World's Best Eco-Lodges and Earth Friendly Hotels, a Fodor's travel guide, offers information on one hundred eco-accommodations around the world. *Green Places to Stay,* by Richard Hammond, part of the *Special Places to Stay* series, also lists eco-accommodations around the world. The eco-accommodations listed in these two books tend to be high-end and spectacular.

If you have a pleasant home in a desirable location you may consider a home exchange program. During a home exchange, you trade homes with someone—they stay in your home and you stay in theirs. The use of cars, bikes, and appliances can be included as part of the exchange, as well as cleaning responsibilities. Special preferences, like nonsmoking or pet-free homes, are usually part of the listing information.

As home exchange programs have grown, the exchange options have increased. In some instances, you no longer need to exchange homes at the same time. There are listings for second homes, and travel times are flexible. Some programs also offer rentals and house-sitting options. Some home exchange programs have a general focus, but others are limited to certain groups. For instance, there is a home exchange program for families whose children go to Waldorf-Steiner schools, and there is another program for seniors.

Global home exchange options are available at www.4homex.com for a $39 annual fee. For home exchanges, house-sitting, and rentals, go to www.sabbaticalhomes.com, which is free to view; however, there is a $55 fee to post a listing.

More home exchange options are available at www.homeexchange. com, which charges a $99.95 annual listing and use fee. Also visit www.intervac.com or www.thevacationexchange.com, which charges a $39.95 annual fee.

Seniors might consider specialty exchange options available at www. seniorshomeexchange.com, which charges a three-year fee of $79 or a $100 lifetime fee. Waldorf school affiliates should check out www. wheponline.com, which charges a $50 annual fee.

House-sitting is another accommodation option when traveling; however, it does usually require animal care—including cats, dogs, or farm animals—and/or plant care. This is a great, low-cost option if you like animals and want to be in one place for your stay. It is not the right choice if you plan to travel around. The Mind My House Web site offers an international search for house-sitters. For more information, go to www.mindmyhouse.com. At Worldwide House-sitting, an Australian-based organization, homeowners list for free and house-sitters sign up for a $40 annual fee. For more information, go to www.housesitworld.com. At www.housecarers.com, another Australian-based organization, homeowners also list for free and house-sitters pay a $45 annual fee. The Caretaker's Gazette, at www.caretaker.org, is another resource for potential home-sitters.

For the adventurous and tight-budgeted, there is a fairly new non-profit organization called Couch Surfing. It includes a network of travelers and hosts, and you can bunk on a host's couch (or spare bed) for free. Go to www.couchsurfing.com for more information about safety issues and membership.

The main page at Craigslist provides links to just about any country or major city. Check the housing lists for great short- and long-

It's time for military time. Be prepared to keep time using the 24-hour-clock system, commonly used throughout Europe. The afternoon and evening times can get confusing if you are not paying attention. And it is easy to miss trains and appointments by calculating the time incorrectly. Watch for problems with 14:00 and 16:00! Remember that 14:00 = 2:00pm and 16:00 = 4:00pm

term rentals or sublet options. For more information, go to www.craigslist.org. Usually updated daily or weekly, Sublet.com also offers short-term housing options all over Europe. For more information, go to www.sublet.com.

Based in the Netherlands, the European Centre of Eco Agro Tourism (ECEAT) focuses on farm stays and accommodations that are committed to the conservation of the environment, biodiversity, and supporting local and organic foods. ECEAT offers information on one thousand small organic farms throughout Europe that provide tenting or farmhouse rooms, plus hundreds of environmentally friendly bed-and-breakfasts, apartments, and guesthouses. If you speak Dutch, you will find their Web site useful. ECEAT, Postbox 10899, 1001 EW Amsterdam; Tel: 02 06 68 10 30; Fax: 02 04 63 05 94; E-mail: eceat@eceat.nl; Web site: www.eceat.nl.

European Union Eco Label certifies some accommodations and campsites. For more information, go to www.ecolable-tourism.eu and www.ecocamping.net.

Green Earth Travel is a travel agency catering to vegetarians. They help with cruises, hotels, and tours geared towards vegetarians. For more information, go to www.vegtravel.com.

For home-stays, a grown-up version of the student exchange program, you can explore U.S. Servas. Servas started in 1948 as a worldwide cooperative exchange network of hosts and travelers working to foster peace and cultural understanding. You can purchase a domestic membership for a $50 annual fee, and international travel membership is $85 annually. For an additional $25 fee you can access up to five "host lists" that detail potential hosts in various countries. Stays usually last for three days and two nights unless the host invites you to stay longer. U.S. Servas, 11 John Street, Room 505, New York, NY 10038; Tel: 212-267-0252; E-mail: info@usservas. org; Web site: www.usservas.org.

Federation EIL, the worldwide network of The Experiment in International Living, runs a few different programs, including their Individual Homestay Program. Stays last from one to four weeks. Fees for a one-week stay cost between $200 and $500. Federation EIL, Box 595, 63 Main Street, Putney, VT 05346; Tel: 802-387-4210; E-mail: fedinfo@experiment.org; Web site: www.experiment.org.

EATING

The Slow Food Network is a nonprofit organization promoting what they term "good, clean, and fair" food. The Slow Food movement embraces healthy and local food, prepared with attention and consideration. The movement is growing worldwide, and many countries have their own Slow Food networks with Web sites. The international site can be found at www.slowfood.com.

The International Vegetarian Union (IVU) has a Web site with helpful but limited information about vegetarian restaurants and hotels in Europe. More information can be found at www.ivu.org. The Happy Cow also maintains an international database of vegetarian restaurants around the world. For more information, go to www. happycow.net.

SHOPPING

Except in large cities—but sometimes there, too—stores generally close between noon and 2:00pm. The specific times will vary per town and country. These are the hours when the shopkeepers, and you, need a break. Get into the swing of it! It is refreshing and delightful to know that everyone has closed up shop and is relaxing and eating, walking or playing.

When shopping, don't forget to bring your own bags. Many stores either do not have bags or charge for flimsy ones. Keep a stash of canvas or reusable bags rolled up in your daypack.

For recycled goods, you can try joining the local FreeCycle group. FreeCycle is an Internet bulletin board exchange where people barter

When buying fresh produce in many places in Europe, you are responsible for weighing and pricing it. You will find a number by the name of the item—Red Cabbage #62, for instance. Take your red cabbage over to the electronic scale, and weigh it, punching in number 62. The machine will spit out a sticker, with the weight and price, which you then affix to the bag or item. In low-tech stores with no sticker machines, simply write the price on the bag.

things they no longer need or want. No money changes hands. At the Web site, you can access almost every state and many countries, including Spain and France. Joining the group makes sense only if you are going to be in one area for a decent length of time. More information can be found at www.freecycle.org.

VOLUNTEER TOURISM

Volunteers for Peace (VFP), founded in 1982, is a nonprofit organization specializing in short-term (two to three weeks) volunteer opportunities around the world for all ages. They have projects in over one hundred countries. Basic registration is $300 per project, and there is a $30 annual membership fee. Other expenses include airfare to your destination and sometimes an additional fee for the project (depending on your destination). The types of projects vary, and there are options for all skill levels and interests. A full project directory and helpful travel links can be found at the VFP Web site. Volunteers for Peace, 1034 Tiffany Road, Belmont, VT 05730-0202; Tel: 802-259-2759; E-mail: vfp@vfp.org; Web site: www.vfp.org.

Peaceful World Travel is a network of people and places all over the world that welcomes travelers and neighbors to participate in peace-building activities and to engage in conversations on matters of local and global peacemaking. Peaceful World Travel is working to create a global network of alternative travel resources, accessible to local and international travelers and hosts, with an emphasis on bed-and-breakfasts, cafés, hostels, and small hotels. Peaceful World Foundation International, 1665 Haight Street, San Francisco, CA 94117; Tel: 415-864-1978; Fax: 415-863-3293; E-mail: peacefulworldtravel@ redvic.com; Web site: www.redvic.com or peacefulworldfoundation. org.

For organic farming opportunities, explore WWOOF—World Wide Opportunities on Organic Farms—an international association with twenty-five member countries and another fifty independent member farms. Each affiliated country has their own association that requires membership. The fee is low, usually in the $25 range. Membership provides you access to the list of participating farms. You choose the farms where you would like to work, make contact with them, and make all of your arrangements. The association does not handle any of the arrangements but does offer tips on the Web sites for maximizing your contact and experience. These are not paid jobs, but rather organic farming work experiences. You and the host farm reach your own agreement about how many hours per day or week you will work in exchange for room, breakfast, and sometimes other meals.

Volunteers for International Partnership, part of The Experiment in International Living, offers volunteer projects in sixteen countries. Fees depend on length of stay and location. For more information, go to www.partnershipvolunteers.org.

Helpful Books

Volunteer Vacations: Short Term Adventures That Will Benefit You and Others, Ninth Edition, by Bill McMillon, Doug Cutchins, and Anne Geissinger. Chicago Review Press, 2006.

Volunteer: A Traveler's Guide to Making a Difference Around the World, by Charlotte Hindle. Lonely Planet, 2007.

Alternatives to the Peace Corps: A Directory of Global Volunteer Opportunities, Revised Edition, by Paul Backhurst. Food First, 2005.

UNITED NATIONS WORLD HERITAGE CENTER

All the World Heritage sites in the world, searchable by country and type, can be found at whc.unesco.org.

SACRED SITES

Extensive information and links to megalith sites can be found at www.stonepages.com.

The Megalithic Portal includes a searchable map of megalithic sites in Europe. For more information, go to www.megalithic.co.uk.

The travel guide available at Sacred Destinations provides information about sacred sites and ancient wonders around the world. For more information, go to www.sacred-destinations.com.

three traveling naturally in France

France is a wonderful mixture of the gritty, dirty, delightful, and friendly, with divine sights, scents, and tastes. It is a country that fills the senses—lovers by the score kissing in the parks, people looking as if they smoke and drink too much, delightful smells and foul odors, and lots of dog *merde* on the streets. Hygiene is not a strong suit, but this is part of what makes it all so … well … French!

France is one of the largest European countries, rich with a variety of agriculture, which makes fresh, local food plentiful. Some of the most delicious food and wine can be found in France. Slow, local, and fresh foods are intrinsic to the French culture. Mindful eating is not a fad or trend. Young children are instructed about taste and quality, not food pyramids, in their school nutrition classes.

While the French have a reputation for being snobby about foreigners who try to speak French, I have found people in France, for the most part, to be friendly, helpful, and forgiving when I butcher their language. Most people seem appreciative that I am making an effort. That said, sometimes the very best thing to do is to ask, *"Parlez-vous anglais?"* and hope for a "Yes."

The French are famous for smoking profusely, and the reputation is fairly justified. Surprisingly, the French are complying with recent no-smoking laws, which means you will not find smoking on public transportation, in public areas, and in many restaurants.

When shopping for local products, especially at the markets, make sure you read the labels, as France is not immune to the temptation

22 Regions of France

Region	Capital	Depts w/in Regions
Alsace	Strasbourg	67, 68
Aquitaine	Bordeux	24,33,40,47,64
Auvergne	Clermont-Ferrand	3,15,43,63
Basse Normandie (Lower)	Caen	14,50,61
Bourgogne - Burgundy	Dijon	21,58,71,89
Bretagne – Brittany	Rennes	22,29,35,56
Centre	Orleans	18,28,36,37,41,45
Champagne-Ardenne	Reims	8,10,51,52
Corsica (Island)	Ajaccio	20b, 20a
Franche Comte	Besancon	25,39,70,90
Haute Normandie (Upper)	Rouen	27,76
Languedoc Roussillon	Montpellier	11,30,34,48,66
Limousin	Limoges	19,23,87
Lorraine	Metz	54,55,57,88
Midi Pyrenees	Toulouse	9,12,31,32,46,65,81,82
Nord Pas de Calais	Lille	59,62
Pays de la Loire	Nantes	44,49,53,72,85
Picardie	Amiens	2,60,80
Poitou Charentes	Poitiers	16,17,79,86
Provence-Alpes-Cote d'Azur	Marseille	4,5,6,13,83,84
Region Parisienne/ Isle de France	Paris	75,77,78,91,92,93,94,95
Rhone Alps	Lyon	1,7,26,38,42,69,73,74

of importing less expensive goods. It would be a shame to learn that your "local," brightly colored Provencal tablecloth, purchased as a souvenir, was actually made in China.

Alternative medicine is popular in France, and, as in other European countries, it is not necessarily considered "alternative." Drugstores often sell herbal and homeopathic remedies alongside pharmaceuticals. There are also numerous specialty pharmacies, especially in the cities, which focus on homeopathic or herbal remedies. In every region of France you will find spas, health centers, and practitioners of all healing modalities.

While there are many differences between the French and other people, there are far more similarities— men stand and watch construction sites, parents love their children, men and women want to enjoy life and be at peace in the world, people complain about taxes and the government. They laugh and cry, starve and feast.

France is an easy country in which to travel naturally and lightly. It has a strong and growing organic agriculture movement, abundant natural scents and body-care products, readily accessible bicycling and hiking, public transportation, and vast natural resources. Enjoy it all!

Orientation, Arrival, and Getting Around

France has a rich history of creative, brilliant, and progressive people, some of whom are well known, others who are not. A short list would have to include Simone de Beauvoir, author and feminist; Jean Piaget, psychologist; Claude Bernard, considered the father of physiology; Antoine Béchamp, pleomorphic and terrain theory biologist; Louis Claude Vincent, the hydrologist who developed Biological Terrain Assessment health testing; Gaston Naessens, pleomorphic

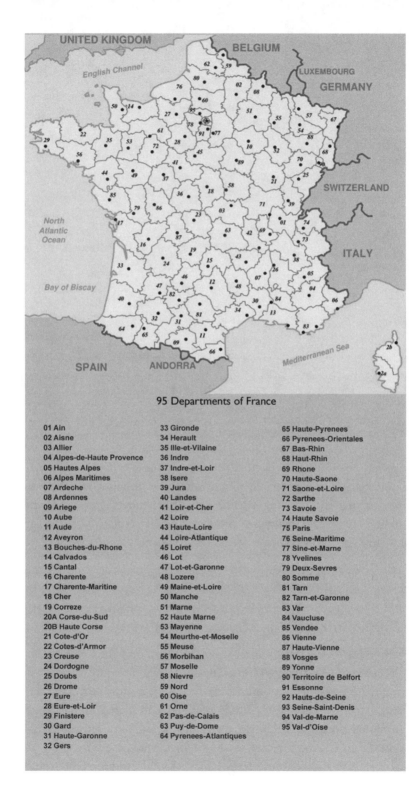

95 Departments of France

01 Ain
02 Aisne
03 Allier
04 Alpes-de-Haute Provence
05 Hautes Alpes
06 Alpes Maritimes
07 Ardeche
08 Ardennes
09 Ariege
10 Aube
11 Aude
12 Aveyron
13 Bouches-du-Rhone
14 Calvados
15 Cantal
16 Charente
17 Charente-Maritine
18 Cher
19 Correze
20A Corse-du-Sud
20B Haute Corse
21 Cote-d'Or
22 Cotes-d'Armor
23 Creuse
24 Dordogne
25 Doubs
26 Drome
27 Eure
28 Eure-et-Loir
29 Finistere
30 Gard
31 Haute-Garonne
32 Gers

33 Gironde
34 Herault
35 Ille-et-Vilaine
36 Indre
37 Indre-et-Loir
38 Isere
39 Jura
40 Landes
41 Loir-et-Cher
42 Loire
43 Haute-Loire
44 Loire-Atlantique
45 Loiret
46 Lot
47 Lot-et-Garonne
48 Lozere
49 Maine-et-Loire
50 Manche
51 Marne
52 Haute Marne
53 Mayenne
54 Meurthe-et-Moselle
55 Meuse
56 Morbihan
57 Moselle
58 Nievre
59 Nord
60 Oise
61 Orne
62 Pas-de-Calais
63 Puy-de-Dome
64 Pyrenees-Atlantiques

65 Haute-Pyrenees
66 Pyrenees-Orientales
67 Bas-Rhin
68 Haut-Rhin
69 Rhone
70 Haute-Saone
71 Saone-et-Loire
72 Sarthe
73 Savoie
74 Haute Savoie
75 Paris
76 Seine-Maritime
77 Sine-et-Marne
78 Yvelines
79 Deux-Sevres
80 Somme
81 Tarn
82 Tarn-et-Garonne
83 Var
84 Vaucluse
85 Vendee
86 Vienne
87 Haute-Vienne
88 Vosges
89 Yonne
90 Territoire de Belfort
91 Essonne
92 Hauts-de-Seine
93 Seine-Saint-Denis
94 Val-de-Marne
95 Val-d'Oise

June 15th through September 16th is considered peak travel time in France. When making plans, take this into consideration. During this period, things will be harder to book, much more crowded, and substantially more expensive.

theory biologist; Emile Zola, author and activist; Voltaire, writer and philosopher; and Albert Camus, writer and philosopher.

July 14th is Bastille Day, a national holiday in France. It is celebrated much like July 4th in the United States. Bastille Day commemorates the storming of the Bastille prison, which ignited the French Revolution, much like the signing of the Declaration of Independence marked the beginning of the American Revolution. The storming of the prison, while slightly less diplomatic than a written document signed by appointed representatives, signified the power of ordinary people against the throne of unjust King Louis XVI, resulting in the French revolution and, eventually, a new form of government. The three colors of the French flag represent the three ideals of the French Republic: *Liberté, Égalité, Fraternité* (Liberty, Equality, Fraternity). These words are inscribed on many buildings in France.

The French are quite famous for their protest strikes, which can cut off electricity, stop transportation, and shut down whole parts of the country. As a traveler, this can be extremely inconvenient, especially if you happen to be caught in a transportation strike. If you do find yourself caught in a strike, try to keep a positive perspective. Strikes are democracy in action, allowing the voice of the people to be heard. France is one of the few countries in the world where strikes are legal and effective. While you are missing your connections and wondering how you will manage, try to appreciate that the French can and do exercise their right to protest.

France has twenty-two regions, subdivided into ninety-five administrative *départements*. Each region and each *département* has a capital. The *départements* are numbered, alphabetically, which makes reading maps and referencing easier. Many French Internet sites will offer searches by *département* number. The city of Paris is arranged into twenty districts called arrondissements. They are like neighborhoods,

JANUARY

- The International Congress of Professionals promotes natural products in cosmetics: www.cosmethica-grasse.com.

FEBRUARY

- The Nice Carnival is held the last two weeks in February: www.nicecarnival.com.

APRIL

- Slow Food Expo in Montpellier is held in mid-April every odd-numbered year: www.slowfood.fr and www.auxoriginesdugout.com.

- Aromatherapy & Medicinal Plant Symposium in Grasse is held during a weekend in mid-April: www.ville-grasse.fr/aromatherapie/uk/home.htm.

- Venusia Beauty & Wellness is held on a weekend in early April in Grasse: www.ville-grasse.fr/venusia/default.htm.

MAY

- The Rose Expo is held in Grasse: www.ville-grasse.fr/exporose.

JUNE

Note: June 15–September 16 are peak travel times.

- Salon Bionazur is the organic products fair & conference in Nice, held over a weekend in mid-June in the Jardin Albert by the Promenade d'Anglais held. The Salon is free and open 10am to 8pm each day: www.bionazur.com.

JULY

- Bayeux Medieval Festival *(Fêtes Médiévales de Bayeux)* is held the first weekend in July.

- Bastille Day—July 14th—is a national holiday, celebrated much like July 4th in the U.S.

- The Tour de France is the world-famous bike race held annually during the last three weeks in July.

- Avignon Theatre and Fringe Festivals are held annually during three weeks in July.

- Les Nuits Musicales de Nice are outdoor classical recitals held throughout Nice in July & August: concerts.hexagone.net/music/nuits_musicales.htm.

- Since 1948 the Nice Jazz Festival has filled the city with music, from ticketed venues to free music concerts, and is held annually in mid-July: www.nicejazzfestival.fr.
- Sacred Music Festival by La Toison d'Art in Paris is held during July & August: www.latoisondart.com.
- Outdoor films in the Prairie du Triangle in Villette Park, Paris, are called the Festival de Cinéma en Plein Air, and are held during July and August. Schedule of films: www.cinema.arbo.com; Park map and information: www.villette.com.

AUGUST
- Sault Lavender Festival is held annually in mid-August.
- Jasmine Festival in Grasse is held the first weekend in August: www.ville-grasse.fr/jasminade/default.htm.
- Mirabelle Festival celebrates a type of plum renowned in the Lorraine region of France. The festival, held since 1947, celebrates all things Mirabelle. The festival runs annually from the end of August to the beginning of September.

SEPTEMBER
- Les Vendanges is the grape harvest held during September and October, depending on the region.
- Bio-Grasse is an organic products festival in Grasse: www.ville-grasse.fr/biograsse/default.htm.
- Mirabelle Festival (see more under **August**).

OCTOBER
- The Ethical Fashion Show is held annually in mid-October in Paris: www.ethicalfashionshow.com.
- International Congress of Professionals promotes natural products in perfumery and is held in Grasse: www.centifolia-grasse.net.

DECEMBER
- Christmas markets are traditional and popular in many cities and villages throughout France. Metz, Lorraine, is especially known for its fantastic Christmas market with over eighty stalls.
- Les Musicales de Décembre by La Toison d'Art: www.latoisondart.com.

but arrondissement numbers do not necessarily correlate to named neighborhoods, such as the Latin Quarter. The Paris zip codes contain the arrondissement number in the last two digits of the zip code. All Paris zip codes begin with 750, so the last two numbers identify the arrondissement. For example, 75004 is in the 4th arrondissement, or 4e as it is sometimes abbreviated. See the *Green Earth Guide* Map of Regions of France and the *Green Earth Guide* Map of Departments of France on pages 23 and 24.

COMMUNICATION

French is spoken everywhere, and, in the Alsace region, German and Alsatian are spoken as well.

Tabac stores (newsstands) in France can sell up to three different kinds of phone cards—one for pay phones and phone booths, another for mobile cell phone use, and the third for long-distance calls from landlines. Sometimes there is an all-in-one card, but these do not always offer the best rates. Make sure you are buying the type of phone card you need.

If you are staying in Paris, it is very helpful to purchase a Guide des Arrondissements, which is sold at tabac stores in Paris for about 9 euros. The guide covers the twenty different arrondissements of Paris, and includes maps and other useful information. Used by locals and tourists alike the red Paris Classique has invaluable detailed maps, street indexes, bus routes, site indexes with metro stops, and more.

If you are using a cell phone, beware the roaming and international fees. Please check with your provider before leaving the United States to avoid bill-shock when you return home.

Printed phone books can be hard to find. Online phone directories for France can be found at www.pagesjaunes.fr (both yellow and white pages) and www.annu.com. To call French phone numbers from the United States, begin by dialing 011 and France's country code 33. From within France, just dial 0 before the phone number.

PUBLIC TRANSPORTATION

The Charles de Gaulle airport is the main airport in Paris, located northeast of the city, and it has bus and train service into the city. The Orly airport, south of Paris, has bus service into the city.

The French word for station is *gare,* and in Paris you will find six

On most trains, your ticket must be validated before boarding. Validate your tickets at the little yellow box-like machines at the end of the platforms. Also, confirm you are boarding the right train by matching the train number on your ticket to the one on the track sign.

Many tickets are for reserved seats. Your ticket will list the train number, coach number, and seat number. You can figure out where to wait on the platform by using the coach locators, which display an illustration of the train, including coach/car numbers, and correlating them to letters on the platform. For example, if you are in coach number 19, the diagram may indicate that you should wait at the "C" area of the platform. On the SNCF tickets, the train number and name (if it has one) will be listed under "Cities."

The following translations may help you make sense of your ticket:

Classe 2 = Second or tourist class

Classe 1 = First class

Couloir or *Corridor* = Aisle seat

Fenêtre = Window seat

Place Assise = Seat

Voie = Track

Voiture = Coach/Car

train stations: Gare de Lyon, Gare du Nord, Gare d'Austerlitz, Gare de l'Est, Gare Montparnasse, and Gare Saint-Lazare. The stations are in different parts of the city and serve various destinations. Gare du Nord is large and busy, orchestrating many trains and housing the Eurostar terminal. The Eurostar is the two-and-a-half-hour high-speed train to London. If you happen to be taking this train, be prepared: the security is as tight or tighter than airport security.

The Paris metro system is extensive, covering every part of the city. Each metro or bus trip costs 1.50 euros. Cost depends on the zone, but most sites are within zone 1. If you want to hop on and off during the day, the most convenient and economical option is to purchase a one-day tourist pass for 8.50 euros. You can get around Paris by bus, too. To download a high-quality metro map and find information for all Paris transportation, go to www.ratp.fr/.

Le Batobus, a boat-bus that travels on the Seine, is a fun way to see the city. Le Batobus makes eight stops, at Tour Eiffel, Musée d'Orsay, Saint-Germain-des-Prés, Notre Dame, Jardin des Plantes, Champs-Élysées, Louvre, and Hôtel de Ville. An unlimited-ride day pass costs 12 euros for an adult and 6 euros for children under 16. Tickets are available at each stop. For more information, go to www.batobus.com/english/index.htm.

Buses, trams, and metros are available in other large cities. Cyclopolitain, a fleet of hybrid electric-peddle-powered tricycle taxis, provide low-cost, ecofriendly transportation. Cities with cyclopolitain taxis include Nice, Lyon, Nantes, Grenoble, Paris, Toulouse, Reims, Rennes, Bourg en Bresse, and Annecy. You can find local phone numbers for reservations at the main Web site. For more information, go to www.cyclopolitain.com.

The comprehensive Web site for French rail, the Société Nationale des Chemins de fer Français—commonly referred to by the initials SNCF—can be found at www.sncf.com. For English, click on the British flag at the bottom left of the page and then navigate to the schedules. Some trains run only on certain days, and fares can vary. When traveling and searching for schedules, the day of the week matters.

Do not be frustrated by the automatic ticket machines in the train stations. While they claim to take credit cards, I have been in many different French rail stations where no card in my wallet would work. I would panic, thinking I had no money left or that the banks had shut me down, only to find at the counter that all of my cards worked perfectly. I finally learned that it was easier to wait in line and buy the ticket from a teller. Some of the tellers speak English, but not all of them. If you know your train and time, it is best to write it out clearly for the teller before getting to the window. Remember to use the 24-hour-clock system for your departure and arrival times.

There are local trains and buses in most regions and cities in France. In Provence, a local train runs between Nice and Digne-les-Bains, making ten stops four times daily. The Chemins de fer de Provence Web site can be found at www.trainprovence.com.

A word of caution about French buses: The buses are not part of a national system. They are operated by different companies in differ-

Be prepared with euro coins for lockers at the held baggage or "left lug-gage" areas. The Paris Gare du Nord left-luggage area does have a change machine, but take a lesson from me: Do not depend on change machines. Sometimes they are out of order, and to get change you will have to exit and then go through security all over again—*un peu* (or *grande*) *de problème!*

ent regions. In most cases, you pay for your fare when you board the bus, but this does not mean the driver will automatically remember your stop. By relying on the driver, I have missed stops and ended up in the wrong villages. I don't know if the drivers do this on purpose or if they simply are not paying attention, but friends who live in Provence say the local bus drivers have trifled with the locals by pass-ing bus stops, seemingly on purpose. Furthermore, many bus stops are nothing more than a curbside drop without signs. Try to be pre-pared—ask if there is a bus schedule, so you know which stops come before yours, and most importantly, ask the bus driver to please an-nounce your stop. As you disembark, make sure it is indeed the place you want to be. To ask, "Can you announce my stop please?" in French, attempt your best accent and say, "Pouvez-vous annoncer mon arrêt, s'il vous plait?" The phonetic pronunciation is "Puvay-vu anunsay mon arret, see vu play?"

The French equivalent of Mapquest—Mappy—is available in thir-teen languages. In addition to the usual options for directions and maps, Mappy also provides information about public transportation schedules. For more information, go to www.iti.fr.

BIKE RENTALS

Paris is a bike-friendly city with over 230 miles of bike lanes. Paris Re-spire (Paris Breathes) was established by the Paris City Council to en-courage bicyclists and pedestrians by limiting traffic on Sundays and public holidays in fourteen areas, including along the Seine River.

Paris, Lyon, Montpellier, and other cities have inexpensive bike rental services. You will find 750 Vélib' stations in Paris, where bikes can be easily picked up or dropped off. Renters need to be fourteen years or older and at least five feet tall. You need to provide your own helmet. A day pass costs 1 euro, and a seven-day pass sells for 5 euros. The full-year pass costs only 29 euros. These prices assume you use the bike for no more than thirty minutes. Additional charges apply for every extra half hour you have the bike. If you want a one- or seven-day pass, have your credit card ready for the automatic ticket machines at the Vélib' stations. (All passes are subject to 150-euro refundable deposit.) For a one-year pass, apply online at www.velib.paris.fr. If you want the same bike for an extended stay, it may be less expensive to use Velo-Rent-a-Bike. For more information, go to www.paris-velo-rent-a-bike.fr/index-gb.php.

In Montpellier the bike rental program is called Vélomagg', and it is similar to Paris's Vélib'. The central Vélomagg' station is located at 27 rue Maguelone. For information, go to www.montpellier-agglo.com/tam/page.php?id_rubrique=273&id_fichier=603.

In Lyon, the bike program is called Vélo'V Grand Lyon, and it operates much like the ones in Paris and Montpellier. More information can be found at the www.velov.grandlyon.com.

In Nantes, France's sixth largest city, Bicloo has seventy-nine pick up points and seven hundred bicycles. Nantes also rents a NGE Ville à Vélo for the full day or longer, inexpensive bike rentals. More information is available at www.nge-nantes.fr/velo00.php.

Accommodations

The following accommodations meet at least one of the *Green Earth Guide* Accommodations criteria (see more under *Green Earth Guide* Accommodations). Lodgings listed under the Eco-Accommodations section specifically and intentionally incorporate multiple ecological practices into their facilities.

HOSTELS

For people traveling alone or in pairs, hostels are one of the least expensive options because you are paying per bed, not per room. Hostels associated with the Hostelling International network can be found at www.fuaj.fr, the Web site for youth hostels in France. This site, available in English and French, lists about 140 hostels throughout France. The Hostelling International main site, searchable by country, can be found at www.hihostels.com. Independent hostels can be found at the international Web site www.backpackers-planet.com, which is also searchable by country.

CAMPING

France boasts 11,000 campsites, more than any other country in Europe. Sites include tent, hut, caravan, RV, and mobile home units. At www.campingfrance.com and www.abccamping.com, information is available in French, English, German, and Spanish. Both sites are searchable by region. Check www.campings-nature.com for special eco-experiences, including Huttopia, which features very low-cost tent-camping options and more expensive rentals in untreated wood shelters in idyllic Rillé, Versailles, and Rambouillet locations. For more details, go to www.huttopia.com. Camping Indigo operates in Lyon, Royat, Forcalquier, Noirmoutier, and Rieumontagné, and rents out mobile homes, tents, Gitotel huts and untreated huts, as well as tent sites, or "pitches," for those with their own equipment. More details can be found at www.camping-indigo.com.

GUESTHOUSES AND BED-AND-BREAKFASTS

Lovely and reasonably priced, guesthouses and bed-and-breakfasts are plentiful throughout France. Breakfast is often included with the nightly fee. For information about bed-and-breakfasts, go to www.bed-breakfast-france.com, www.bed-and-breakfast.la-france.org, and www.chambresdhotes.fr. For guesthouses, go to www.gites-de-france.com, which lists over 56,000 rural *gîtes,* bed-and-breakfasts, and camping options throughout France. The Web site is searchable by region, town, or date. For Paris specifically, see the Paris bed-and-breakfast Web page at www.parisbandb.com.

Château de Rosieres, a *chambre d'hôte* (bed-and-breakfast) in Burgundy, is a renovated small castle and farm. On this working farm, twenty-five miles northeast of Dijon and three hours east of Paris, there are four rooms in the renovated fifteenth-century castle, ranging in price from 60 euros a night for two people to 150 euros a night for four people. Meals are available for an extra price. You can also take tours of the castle and grounds if you are not a guest. Château de Rosieres, Mr. and Mrs. Bergerot, Saint-Seine-sur-Vingeanne, 21610, Fontaine Francaise; Tel: 03 80 75 96 24; E-mail: rosieresbb@aol.com; Web site: www.chateauderosieres.com.

Chambre d'hôte Comptoir d'Aubrac is a rural and eclectic bed-and-breakfast. The building that houses the hotel was built in 1862 for pilgrims on their way to Santiago de Compostela in Spain—the route passes in front of the hotel. For more information about the Santiago routes, see the Sacred Sites section. There are six guest rooms and a yurt in the garden. Catherine Painvin, Saint-Chély, d'Aubrac; Tel: 05 65 48 78 84; E-mail: comptoir.aubrac@tiscali.fr; Web site: www.catherinepainvincouture.com.

The Spring Farm, or Ferme de la Source, is a guesthouse with four bedrooms in a stone farmhouse that has been renovated with natural materials. The hot water is heated from solar collectors, and the farm serves local and organic food. Rooms range from 50 to 55 euros a night. Ferme de la Source, le Village, F-26150 Ponet Saint-Auban (near Die); Tel: 03 34 75 22 02 98; E-mail: duriez-francoise@wanadoo.fr; Web site: www.fermedelasource.com/eng.

Nearby in Sainte-Croix, Le Domaine Achard-Vincent offers tastings of *bio* Clairette, the local sparkling wine. For more information, call 04 75 21 20 73. You can find an organic herb farm and a local essential oil distillery nearby, too. The Die market is open on Wednesday and Saturday mornings, and has lots of local and *bio* foods.

The beautiful and very special Les Olivettes bed-and-breakfast villa, with individual apartments, is located in the picturesque village of Lourmarin in Provence. Les Olivettes is within walking distance of the village center, across the main road, and has lovely grounds filled with gardens and olive trees—hence the name. In fact, if you visit during olive harvest time you can help pick the olives. Les Olivettes is not a budget accommodation, but rather a reasonably priced luxury accommodation, beautifully appointed. Les Olivettes, Ave. Henri Bosco, Lourmarin; Tel: 04 90 68 03 52; E-mail: j.deliso@olivettes.com; Web site: www.olivettes.com.

HOME EXCHANGE AND HOUSE-SITTING

For home exchange, house-sitting, and sublet possibilities, see Europe-wide Information and Resources. Some spas and clinics in France have accommodation facilities, others are only available for outpatient or day spa use. See the Health section for detailed spa and clinic information.

ECO-ACCOMMODATIONS

La Clef Verte (The Green Key) is a French organization that certifies establishments based on their environmental commitments. For more information, go to www.laclefverte.org. Under "Touriste," click on "Le Palmares liste" for a list of certified establishments, which include 161 camping areas and twelve hotels and guesthouses. The "carte" choice lets you click on a map to select a region.

L'Orri de Planès, in Southern France along the Trans-Pyrénées walking trails, is a definite winner in terms of ecostandards. They have solar electricity and hot water, and a solar-heated pool. They serve local and organic food, and maintain a very strong environmental commitment. L'Orri de Planès, Cases del Mitg, 66210, Planès; Tel: 04 68 04 29 47; Cell: 06 22 32 25 32; E-mail: contact@orrideplanes.com; Web site: www.orrideplanes.com.

The Hôtel Les Goëlands, located only two minutes from the beach, uses recycled toilet paper, ecodetergents, and has gardens and sea views. The town of Saint-Jean-de-Luz offers a beach and thalassotherapy center. Hôtel Les Goëlands, 4 et 6 Avenue d'Etcheverry, 64500, Saint-Jean-de-Luz; Tel: 03 35 59 26 10 05; Fax: 03 35 59 51 04 02; E-mail: reception@hotel-lesgoelands.com; Web site: www.hotel-lesgoelands.com.

Maison Angéline is a guesthouse with an organic garden and Green Key certification. It is accessible from the Grandes Randonnées hiking path (GR5). Maison Angéline, 5 Grand rue, Arry; Tel: 03 87 52 83 95; Mossele, Lorraine; Web site: www.maison-angeline.com.

Le Cadran Solaire is a bed-and-breakfast that serves local and *bio* foods. It has a Green Key certification, an efficient washing machine, and is surrounded by vineyards and oak trees. Le Cadran Solaire, Route des Crozes, F-34800 Cabrières; Tel: 04 67 88 19 44; Web site: www.le-cadran-solaire.fr/e_introduction.html.

Hôtel les Orangeries, an E.U. EcoLabel-certified hotel, serves local food and uses renewable energy. Prices range from 65 to185 euros per night, depending on the season and size of the room. Hôtel les

Orangeries, 12 avenue du Docteur Dupont, 86320, Lussac-les-Châteaux; Tel: 05 49 84 07 07; E-mail: orangeries@wanadoo.fr; Web site: www.lesorangeries.fr.

Les Cygnes Holiday Homes is a rent-by-the-week *gîte,* ranging from 650 to 2000 euros a week depending on the size of your party and the season. You are expected to bring your own linens and towels, or pay extra for them. There are three houses available, which house six, eight, or ten people, as well as a converted barn and a saltwater swimming pool. Les Cygnes recycles, composts, uses rain water collection, plants trees, and is working on energy self-sufficiency and energy conservation measures. They consider themselves to be carbon neutral. Les Cygnes Holiday Homes, 14 rue des Gregnolets Le Breuil Coiffard; Tel: 05 49 07 47 84; E-mail: info@lescygnes.net; Web site: www.lescygnes.net.

Domaine de Saint-Géry, in Southwest France near Cahors, is an Ecoclub member. The luxurious guesthouse sits amidst sixty-five hectares of nature preserve with organic truffle grounds. Local and organic food is served. At 200 to 400 euros a night, it is not for the budget-minded. Domaine de Saint Géry, 46800 Montaug en Queray; Tel: 05 65 31 82 51; Web site: www.saint-gery.com.

Twelve yurts comprise the hotel Canvas Chic, located by the Ardèche river gorge in the Rhones-Alp region of southern France. Open from mid-April through October, rates for a three-night minimum stay with breakfast range from 255 to 300 euros for two adults, depending on the season. Canvas Chic, Labastide de Virac, Ardèche, Tel: 04 66 24 21 81; E-mail: info@canvaschic.com; Web site: www.canvaschic.com.

L'Arc is a bed-and-breakfast in the Brittany region, serving vegetarian and organic food, and offering therapeutic massage and yoga. The bed-and-breakfast accommodations cost 39 euros per person/per night. Dinners cost 16 to 22 euros, depending on the number of courses. They offer a special three-night romantic package for 275 euros per person, with champagne and homemade chocolates, candlelit dinners, complementary wine, and massage treatments. The closest train station is in Pontivy, about twenty minutes away. L'Arc en Ciel, Guernendalen, Langoelan, Brittany; Tel: 02 97 51 24 05; E-mail: enquiries@vegetarianfrance.com; Web site: www.vegetarianfrance.com.

The Hi Hôtel in Nice is a modern luxury hotel that does not permit smoking. They serve organic food, provide Wi-Fi, and maintain a spa with a steam bath. Prices range from 215 to 690 euros, depending on room or suite occupancy. Hi Hôtel, 3 Avenue des Fleurs; Tel: 04 97 07 26 26; E-mail: hi@hi-hotel.net; Web sites: www.hi-hotel.net and www.myspace.com/hihotel/.

La Maison du Vert is a small, vegetarian hotel and restaurant with three guest rooms. The red brick building, originally the village bakery, is surrounded by over two acres of organic gardens with outdoor seating for dining in nice weather. They serve organic food from their own gardens, as well as local organic wine, cider, and beer. La Maison du Vert, Ticheville, Vimoutiers, Normandy; Tel: 02 33 36 95 84; E-mail: info@maisonduvert.com; Web site: www.maisonduvert.com.

Laroche is a bed-and-breakfast and self-catering *gîte* set amidst five acres of gardens and natural beauty. Near the villages of Brantome and Villars, Laroche is an affordable lodging with prices ranging from 36 euros per person/per night to 80 euros per night for three people. Laroche, Quinsac, Champagnac de Belair, Dordogne; Tel: 05 53 54 22 91; E-mail: allisons@club-internet.fr; Web site: perso.club-internet.fr/allisons.

La Ferme Paulianne, an organic farm with 220 acres in southeast France, offers a range of accommodation options. There are five *gîtes,* three caravans, and one yurt. Tents can be pitched for 2 euros per person/per night. La Ferme Paulianne, Luc-en-Diois; Tel: 04 75 21 37 43; E-mail: paulianne@free.fr.

Georgeanne Brennan is a food writer, cook, and proponent of local, organic foods. Her most recent work, *A Pig in Provence,* focuses on her personal experiences living in Provence over thirty years ago. She writes at length about the local foods of Provence, the southeastern region of France known for its lavender, truffles, herbs, and other delicacies. From April to October, Georgeanne rents out a renovated, two-bedroom stone house in the medieval village of Saint-Martin de-Bromes, forty-five minutes northeast of Aix-en-Provence. She charges $600 per week. You can take in the thermal baths in nearby Greoux-les-Bains. For detailed information and photographs, visit her Web site at www.georgeannebrennan.com/village_house.php.

Perfect for one or two people, Covert Cabin has one double bed. This secluded lodging is off the electrical grid and employs a variety of creative lights. There is a wood stove and an outdoor shower. The cabin is located on six acres on a private lake, five kilometers from Piégut-Pluviers in Perigord Vert, Dordogne. Expect to pay $500 a week. Covert Cabin, Lacaud, Busserolles, Dordogne; Tel: 05 53 56 81 24; E-mail: bobcabin@wanadoo.fr; Web site: www.covertcabin. com.

The Hôtel de la Porte Dorée is a reasonably priced, family-run hotel in Paris that offers environmental considerations such as green cleaning products, recycling bins, and water and energy conservation. The hotel has free Wi-Fi, and all the rooms are nonsmoking. Rates range from 63 to 110 euros per night, and discounts are available for stays of three or more nights. Hôtel de la Porte Dorée, 273 avenue Daumesnil, 75012 Paris; Métro: Porte Doree; Tel: 01 43 07 56 97; Fax: 01 49 28 08 18; Web site: www.hotelportedoree.com.

Eating and Food

Food in France can be amazing. Slow, local, and fresh foods are intrinsic to French culture. Health food stores and markets can be found in almost every town, and every region has specialty foods and organic farms. Stores take a lunch break, lasting one to three hours, and people use this time to share a meal and recharge. On Sundays, stores are closed completely. Monday mornings are virtually dead; even most of the cafés are closed.

While many cafés serve local fare, the many that do not are still part of the local fabric. The French National Federation of Cafés, Brasseries and Discotheques reports that in 1960, France had 200,000 cafés. Due to changing habits and economic downturns, there are less than 41,500 cafés now operating in France. Please make an effort to support local cafés as you wind your way through the back roads and high streets of France.

VEGETARIAN, ORGANIC, AND GLUTEN-FREE CHOICES

In France, organic agriculture is called *agriculture biologique,* or *agriculture bio* for short. Food grown organically is certified as *bio* by one

Organic agriculture involves farming by certain standards, which include and promote environmental sustainability, biodiversity, animal welfare, soil fertility improvement, and high-quality food production. Organic farming is implemented without the use of synthetic pesticides, herbicides, fungicides or fertilizers, genetically modified organism (GMO) seeds, antibiotics, hormones, or processing with irradiation.

Countries have their own organic certification agencies. In Europe, some countries have four agencies, while others have as many as thirty-six different certification organizations monitoring and certifying organic food and other products. The Organic Consumers Association (OCA) is a nonprofit organization in the United States working on many issues, including organic food and sustainable farming. For extensive information and resources, visit the OCA Web site at www.organicconsumers.org.

I like the following books for additional information about organic farming:

Rodale's Illustrated Encyclopedia of Organic Gardening, by Maria Rodale and Pauline Pears. DK Publishing, 2005.

The Grape Grower: A Guide to Organic Viticulture, by Lon Rombough. Chelsea Green Publishing, 2002.

of France's several organic certification organizations. French Organic Federation AB (Agriculture Biologique) and Ecocert labels indicate organically grown food. For more information, see the Web sites www.agencebio.org and www.ecocert.fr. A Demeter label indicates biodynamically grown and produced goods (see a description of biodynamic farming on page 85). Max Havelaar is a fair-trade label. For more information, go to www.maxhavelaarfrance.org.

In many large chain supermarkets, including Monoprix, you can usually find some *bio* foods and local products. Stores that specialize in *bio* foods include La Vie Claire, Biocoop, Bio Generation, and Rendez-vous de la Nature. You can search their Web sites for store locations all over France.

By January 2010, all plastic bags in France must be compostable and bio-degradable. You will notice the new compostable bags by their very different feel. It is always best to bring your own reusable bag or to use a traditional market basket.

Bonne Terre has been developing and distributing *bio* products since 1950. Their Web site is a great resource for locating health food stores around France. Go to www.bonneterre.fr and click on "Trouver un Magasin." The map will allow you to find health food stores in every region of France, including 120 in Paris alone.

Biocoop, with almost three hundred member stores, provides a useful link for health food stores around France. Go to www.biocoop.fr and click on "Magasins Biocoop." Click on any section of the map to get a comprehensive list of the health food stores in the area.

Like the Biocoop, La Vie Claire offers a comprehensive list of stores on their Web site at www.lavieclaire.com. Click on "Nos Magasins" to locate the map. There are twelve stores in Paris and many locations all over the country. Click on the region to find any store address and phone number.

Acheter Bio: Le guide Hachette des produits bio ("The Hachette Guide to Organic Products"), by Philippe Desbrosses, sells for 15 euros in France and lists over two thousand organic producers.

Every odd-numbered year, Slow Food fans can catch the international Slow Food Expo in Montpellier. For more information about this event, go to www.slowfood.fr and www.auxoriginesdugout.com. If you have questions, you can e-mail france@slowfood.fr.

HEALTH FOOD STORES

Paris

La Nature à Paris Boutique Bio Health Food Store is right next door to the Phyto Bar Organic Restaurant. Eat first and shop afterward! Open Monday–Saturday 9:30am to 8:30pm; Sunday 11am to 8:30pm. La Nature à Paris Boutique Bio Health Food Store, 45 boulevard Saint-Germain, 75005 Paris; Tel: 01 43 54 19 16; E-mail: lanatureaparis@wanadoo.fr.

Another La Nature à Paris Boutique Bio Health Food Store is located in the covered market of Saint-Germain. Open Tuesday–Friday 8am to 1pm, 4pm to 8pm; Saturday 8am to 1:30pm, 3:30pm to 8pm; Sunday 8am to 1:30pm. La Nature à Paris Boutique Bio Health Food Store, 4 to 6 rue Lobineau, Paris; Tel: 01 43 25 14 76; E-mail: lanatureaparis@wanadoo.fr.

Bio Saint-Germain is a lovely, bright store filled with *bio* food. Bio Saint Germain, 30 boulevard Saint-Germain, Paris; Tel: 44 07 34 84; Web site: www.biosaintgermain.com.

Boulangerie Poujauran specializes in organic products, including organic baguettes. Open Tuesday–Saturday 8:30am to 8:30pm. Boulangerie Poujauran, 20 rue Jean Nicot, Paris; Métro: La Tour-Maubourg; Tel: 01 47 05 80 88.

Naturalia France is a chain of health food stores with twenty-five locations throughout Paris and three stores dedicated to natural beauty products. For more information, go to www.naturalia.fr. Click on "Trouver notre magasins," and you will be lead to a map and a listing of all their stores, with addresses, in and around Paris.

Avignon

Biotope, a Biocoop store, is a full-service, coop-style health food store, located half a block outside the University old gate. It is tucked back off the street and is fronted by a gravel parking lot. Open Monday–Friday 9:30am to 1pm, 3pm to 7:30pm; Saturday 9am to 3pm. Biotope, 5 route de Lyon, Avignon; Tel: 04 90 85 14 19.

Biotope sells fresh bread and baked goods from bio Le Pain des Moissons (AB certified). Le Pain des Moissons, 36 place Montfort, Vaison-la-Romaine; Tel: 04 90 36 03 25.

Mas de la Santé is a small natural food store that sells health products, including local *bio* hydrosols from the nearby Graveson Distillery (see more details under Aroma). Mas de la Santé, 13 rue Carnot, Avignon; Tel: 04 90 86 10 48.

Boutique Nature sells natural beauty care, cosmetics, supplements, and books. Open Tuesday–Saturday 10am to 5pm; Monday 2pm to

5pm. Boutique Nature, 29 rue du Vieux, Sextier; Tel: 04 32 76 27 39.

Bio Atelier, across from the Shakespeare Livres Anglais (English Books) bookshop, is a tiny health food store run by the owners of Kafezen café. Open Tuesday–Saturday 9:45am to 12:45pm, 4pm to 7pm. Bio Atelier, 132 rue de la Carreterie.

Le Fruitier de Saint-Agricol stocks divine local and organic foods, including excellent cheeses, oils, and produce. Do not miss the to-die-for basil-infused olive oil, made by a secret process that insures the freshest basil flavor. It is owned and run by Vincent, a lovely, informative man. Le Fruitier de Saint-Agricol, 27 rue Saint-Agricol, Avignon; Tel: 04 90 85 83 82; Web site: www.lefruitier.com. ☛ green earth guide favorite.

Stocking produce and dry goods, Avignon-Bio is a tiny store located across from Les Halles Market. Avignon-Bio, rue de la Petite, Meuse; Tel: 04 90 82 46 84.

Le Panier des Amis, in the Les Halles Market, is a tiny *bio* market crammed with organic produce, local bio-wines, juices, and dry goods. Les Halles is only open in the mornings and is closed Mondays. Tuesday–Saturday 7am to 1pm. Le Panier des Amis, in the Les Halles Market, Place Pie; Tel: 04 90 87 14 32.

Eco de la Terre is a fairly large store—located a good distance from the old, walled part of the city—with a wonderful selection of products. Open Monday 3pm to 7pm; Tuesday to Saturday 9:30am to 1pm, 3pm to 7pm. Eco de la Terre, Route de Monfavet; Tel: 04 90 88 44 75.

Nice

La Vie Claire can be found around the corner from the Nice Camelias Youth Hostel, behind the Nice Étoile and Monoprix, in the heart of downtown Nice. This La Vie Claire is a nice, full-service health food store with a large selection of gluten-free products, including palmier pastries. Open Monday–Saturday 9am to 7pm. La Vie Claire has another location in Nice, out by the airport. La Vie Claire, 18 rue Lamartine, Nice; Tel: 04 93 54 85 99; Web site: www.lavieclaire.fr.

Gaia Bio is a sweet, tiny health food store in the heart of the old city, a few blocks from the market square, with local aroma products and a small selection of food. Gaia Bio, rue Jesus, Nice.

Located in a non-touristy part of Nice, Biocoop Azur is a full-service health food store with a generally good selection of products. Take the #7 bus from the old part of the city. If you are looking for gluten-free items, La Vie Claire is the better choice. Biocoop Azur, 59 boulevard Delfino, Nice; Tel: 04 93 56 69 42.

Montpellier

Biotiful is an awesome, small health food store in the old part of city, with a good selection of organic and gluten-free foods, as well as organic cosmetics, aromatherapy, and baby products. Open Monday–Saturday 10am to 7pm. Biotiful, 15 rue Trésoriers de la Bourse, Montpellier; Tel: 04 67 60 22 07; Web site: www.biotiful-montpellier.com.

La Vie Saine, located one block outside the old part of the city, is a full-service health food store with a large selection of everything. This is a truly excellent store. La Vie Saine, Le Grand Marché Bio, 3 rue Castilhon, Montpellier; Tel: 04 67 58 71 54. ☛ green earth guide favorite.

Dolce Natura is a beautiful natural body-care store in the old part of the city. They sell a limited array of food items, including a special *bio* Rose "sherbet" drink made from rose water and apple juice. Dolce Natura, 15 rue des Sœurs Noires, Montpellier; Tel: 04 67 55 38 97; Web site: www.dolce-natura.com.

Alsace

In the Alsace region you can search for health food stores on the Web site of the Alsace professional organic agriculture organization at www.opaba.org. Search under "Membres," "Les members opérateurs," and "Distributeurs."

Provence

At the Bio de Provence Web site you can access very useful guides listing locations of markets, local stores, and producers of organic foods. The green-colored Bio guides are available in print locally or, conveniently, online at www.bio-provence.org/spip.php?rubrique72.

Once there, you can download guides for seven areas: Hautes-Alpes, Vaucluse, Alpes-de-Haute Provence, Alpes-Maritimes, Provence, or Le Var.

Brittany

To locate *bio* foods in Brittany go to the Brittany organic association Web site at www.interbiobretagne.asso.fr/. Once there, click on "Le points de vente" at the left of the page. There you can find or search all the stores and markets selling organic products in the entire region.

Normandy

To locate *bio* foods in Normandy, go to the Normandy Organic Association Web site at www.bio-normandie.org. To download the sixty-eight-page guidebook to organic food in Normandy, click on "Mangez Bio," "Guide de Points de vent," and "Manger Bio en Basse-Normandie." If you click on "La Bio a la carte," you can search by area for *bio* farms, *bio* markets and *bio* stores.

Other Regions

Search the Web sites of the countrywide health food stores listed above for their various store locations throughout France.

At the Agriculture Bio Web site, you can find regional *bio* organizations, with maps and information about producers. For more information, go to www.agriculturebio.org. Once there, click on the map for regional contacts, which sends you to the local Web site. Look for "Carte de Producteurs" to find farmers and stores selling certified organic products.

FARM STANDS, MARKETS, AND LOCAL PRODUCTS

Local produce and products can be found at bakeries, butcher shops, and on farms. In the villages where you are staying, ask at health food stores, bakeries, and butchers to find the local farm stands.

Weekly markets often sell more than just food, so look for market information in the Shopping and Regional Highlights sections. In Paris, there are markets galore. Throughout the twenty arrondissements (districts), there are seventy-eight markets held on varying days of the week. At chocolateandzucchini.com/parismarkets.html you will find a list of all Paris markets, compiled by the city of Paris and refined by Clotilde Dusoulier, under "Markets of Paris." Listed below are the markets that specialize in *biologique* or *bio* (organic) foods.

Marché Biologique Raspail is held on boulevard Raspail between rue du Cherche-Midi and rue de Rennes in the 6th arrondissement every Sunday morning from 9am to 1:30pm. Métro: Sévres-Babylon or Saint-Placide.

The Marché Raspail, held in the same location on Tuesday and Friday mornings, is not considered *biologique*.

Marché Biologique Batignolles is held on boulevard des Batignolles (17e). It is open every Saturday from 9am to 2pm. Métro: Rome.

Marché Biologique Brancusi is held every Saturday morning on Place Constantin in the 14th arrondissement from 9am to 3pm. Métro: Gaité.

You will find a huge Sunday food market with wall-to-wall people and vendors in Nice, Provence. In the heart of the old city, at place Pierre Gautier, the market is full of beautiful food—piles of sun-dried tomatoes, olives, cheeses, flowers, fruits, and vegetables—and it is full of French people doing their Sunday shopping. The *bio* stands are in the back right corner of the market if you have entered through the main gate on the beach side. The produce is abundant, even in the winter. ☛ green earth guide favorite.

At the Bio de Provence Web site you can access very useful guides listing locations of markets, local stores, and producers of organic foods. The green-colored Bio guides are available in print locally or, conveniently, online at www.bio-provence.org/spip.php?rubrique72. Once there, you can download guides to seven areas: Hautes-Alpes, Vaucluse, Alpes-de-Haute-Provence, Alpes-Maritimes, Provence, or Le Var.

You can find similar regional *bio* organizations, with maps and information about producers, at www.agriculturebio.org, the Agriculture Bio Web site. If you click on the map for regional contacts, you can access local Web sites. Search "Carte de Producteurs" to find farmers and stores selling certified organic products. Other regional *bio* organizations are listed in the Health Food Stores section.

Local Specialties

Fresh organic bread from the Boulangerie de l'Hermitage is available in many stores and markets, which are listed under "Points de vente" on their Web site. The bakery itself is inland, west of Saint-Tropez. You will need a car to get there. They make a variety of breads, including kamut and olive loaves. Open 8:45am to 12:30pm, 3:30pm to 6pm. Closed Saturday afternoons and all day Sunday and Monday. Boulangerie de l'Hermitage, Route de Repenti, 83590 Gonfaron, Var; Tel: 04 98 05 10 90; Web site: www.boulangeriehermitage.com.

Truffes de Provence, open all year, sells truffles and offers tastings. Truffle growers also offer demonstrations of truffle digging and hunting. Truffes de Provence, Ferme les Blayos, La Bastide du Clovis, Quartier les Blayos, Gordes; Tel: 04 90 72 11 60; E-mail: Robert.florent84200@orange.fr.

For fresh olives, olive soap, and stone-pressed olive oil from one of the last oil mills in Nice, visit Moulin à Huile Alziari. Open Tuesday–Saturday 8:15am to 12:15pm, 2:15pm to 7pm. Moulin à Huile Alziari, 14 rue Saint-François-de-Paule, Nice; Tel: 04 93 85 72 92.

Enjoy fresh, organic goat cheese in the Drome Valley from Danielle and Jean-Louis Meurot. Danielle and Jean-Louis Meurot, 26150 Vachéres-en-Quint; Tel: 04 75 21 23 77; E-mail: heberge@valleedequint.com; Web site: www.valleedequint.com/producteurs.htm.

A cross between spinach and lettuce, *mache* is a healthy, local green. It is inexpensive and abundant, and available at every health food store, farm stand, and market.

The Les Oleïades, Za la Condamine, and Aouste brands of basil-infused olive oil are simply to die for! For more information, go to www.les-oleiades.com. ☞ green earth guide favorite.

RESTAURANTS

As is true almost everywhere, dining out in France can be very expensive, but reasonably priced meals can be had at some of the vegetarian and *bio* options listed here. Le Pain Quotidien, a Belgian chain restaurant, serves organic and natural foods. To find the France locations in Aix, Lille, Rouen, plus the five locations in Paris, go to www.lepainquotidien.com.

1 Organic market stand, Nice. *Biologique* is the French word for organic.

2 Le Fruitier, purveyor of divine local, organic, gourmet foods, Avignon.

3 Pesto, olive tapenade, lavender sachets, and other market delights.

4 The abundant market in Arles.

5 A bounty of vegetables.

6 Herb stalls common at every market.

7 Garlic, onions, and baguettes.

8 Fresh, organic bread at the market.

9 The Isle-sur-la-Sorgue brocantes market—a veritable gold mine.

10 Fragrant bouquets of flowers and dried lavender.

11 Ochre cliffs in Roussillon.

12 Ochre and other colors electrify Roussillon.

13 Rich colors of ochre seen at sunrise.

14 Natural pigment from the ochre deposits creates vivid façades.

15 Mistletoe in the trees is a very common sight throughout France.

16 Matisse Museum, Nice.

17 Guardians of Arles.

18 The hostel in Bayeux.

19 Vélib, the city-sponsored bike rental program in Paris.

20 Gordes, Provence.

21 Vélomagg', the city-sponsored bike rental program in Montpellier.

22 A Provençal street.

23 Herboristerie herb store in Paris.

24 Shakespeare and Company English bookstore, Paris.

25 Naturalia health food store, one of twenty-five, in Paris.

26 Biotiful, the beautiful health food store, Montpellier.

27 Sandwiches with good olive oil in Arles.

28 Bio & Cie natural foods restaurant, Nice.

29 La Vie Saine health food store in Montpellier.

30 Terre de Saveurs natural foods restaurant, Avignon.

31 La Vie Claire health food store, one of dozens throughout France.

32 One of the three Florame aromatherapy stores in France.

Paris

Billed as the first all-organic bar and restaurant in Paris, Phyto Bar serves terrific organic food. They offer an array of fresh squeezed juices—the grapefruit-kiwi is an especially refreshing combination. The seaweed "caviar," made with a variety of greens from the sea, is highly recommended. Next door, you will find La Nature à Paris Boutique, their sister health food store. Phyto Bar Restaurant and Bar, 47 boulevard Saint-Germain, Paris; Tel: 01 44 07 36 99; E-mail: contact@phytobar.fr; Web site: www.phytobar.fr. ☛ green earth guide favorite.

Bio Art serves organic and local food, and they offer a nice Sunday brunch. Open Monday–Saturday 12pm to 3pm, 7pm to 10:30pm; Sunday 10am to 3pm. Bio Art, 3 Quai François Mauriac, Paris; Tel: 01 45 85 66 88; Web site: www.restaurantbioart.fr.

Au Grain de Folie is a nice organic food restaurant located at 24 rue de La Vieuville in Paris.

Rose Bakery uses organic ingredients in simple dishes—soups, salads, and pastries. Weekend brunch is served, but be cautioned: There is often a line on Sunday mornings. Open 9am to 7pm every day but Monday. Rose Bakery, 46 rue des Martyrs, Paris; Tel: 42 82 12 80.

Le Grenier de Notre Dame is on a side street across the river from Notre Dame, a couple of blocks from the Shakespeare and Company bookstore. Le Grenier serves a variety of delicious vegetarian food with reasonable prices ranging from 6 to 17 euros. Open Monday–Friday 12pm to 2:30pm, 6:30pm to 8:30pm; Saturday–Sunday 12pm to 11pm. Le Grenier de Notre Dame, 18 rue de la Bûcherie, Paris.

Le Puits de Legumes is a vegetarian, organic, and macrobiotic restaurant near the Pantheon. Open 12pm to 10pm, seven days a week. Le Puits de Legumes, 18 rue du Cardinal Lemoine, Paris; Tel: 43 25 50 95; E-mail: lepuitsdelugunes@hotmail.fr.

Visit the Grand Mosque in Paris for a truly unique experience. Built by the French government in the early 1900s as a gesture of gratitude to the North African Muslims who helped defend France, the mosque itself is beautiful in its simplicity, with tiled and whitewashed walls, and gardens. It houses a beautiful restaurant and a tearoom, with indoor and outdoor seating. The outdoor seating area feels like stepping into another world, with blue- and white-tiled tables set amongst trees, plants, and birds. Across the street, you can walk through the Jardins de Plantes, which are filled with medicinal and decorative plants. The infusion menthe (mint tea), made with a handful of fresh mint leaves in a clear glass of hot water, is highly recommended. Inside the mosque you will find the restaurant, the tearoom, a gift store, and a Turkish bath. The Salon de Thé is open seven days a week from 9am to 11:30pm. The restaurant is only open midday and evenings. La Mosquée, 39 rue Geoffroy Saint-Hilaire, Paris; Tel: 43 31 38 14; Web site: www.la-mosquee.com. ☞ green earth guide favorite.

The food may not be organic, but for a simple, inexpensive meal and great conversation, go to the Bouillon Chartier. The restaurant opened in 1896 and caters to solo travelers looking for conversation while dining. People from all nationalities sit together and visit during the meal. One of the restaurant's favorite stories is about a couple who met while dining, fell in love and got married, and returned for their fiftieth anniversary. Entrée prices range from 9 to 21 euros. Open daily 11:30am to 3pm, 6pm to 10pm. Bouillon Chartier, 7 rue du Faubourg Montmartre, 9th arrondissement, Paris; Métro: Grans Boulevards; Tel: 47 70 86 29; Web site: www.restaurant-chartier.com/www/visit/filsdesans.php.

The Afghanistan, owned and run by Afghani chef Sadjia Masshour, serves fresh, ethnic Afghani food. Open Tuesday–Saturday, for dinner only, starting at 7:30pm. The Afghanistan, 48 rue Saint-Maur, Paris; Tel: 01 49 23 02 91.

Avignon

Kafezen Bio is a tiny café with good, cheap *bio* food. Soup and salad goes for 6 euros. The same people operate the Relax Yoga atelier and the little Bio Atelier health food store. Open Monday–Friday. Kafezen Bio, 16 rue Henri Fabre, Avignon; Tel: 04 90 85 93 31.

Serving natural and vegetarian meals, Terre & Saveurs is a nice restaurant in the old part of Avignon. Open Tuesday–Saturday 11:30am to 2pm for lunch; Friday–Saturday 7pm to 9:30pm for dinner. Terre & Saveurs, Place des Corps-Saints, Avignon.

Pan & Cie, located at Place des Corps-Saints, Avignon, is a bakery and sandwich shop featuring organic breads and fresh food.

Vegetarian Paris: Your Guide to Vegetarian Restaurants, by Laure Goldbright, is a tremendously helpful book for travelers wanting to stick to a vegetarian diet in the City of Lights.

Clothilde Dusoulier has a friendly, easy way of conveying the delights and nuances of French food. For five years, her blog, Chocolate and Zucchini, found at chocolateandzucchini.com, has focused on fresh, local, and organic foods. A personal guide through the restaurants, cafés, and markets of Paris, her book *Clothilde's Edible Adventures in Paris* is a must-have guide for anyone traveling to Paris. You will find information on 164 eating establishments, plus 130 listings for bakeries, markets throughout the city, and shops of every kind. Clothilde provides in-depth descriptions of each spot so you can decide which peak your interest. Please note that these are not necessarily organic or vegetarian food stops.

Both books are available through the Traveling Naturally online bookstore, powered by Amazon at astore.amazon.com/travelnaturalgo-20.

The chicken sandwich with mango chutney, almonds, and mesclun greens is delicious.

Nice

With twelve little tables, Bio & Cie is a small restaurant that fills up at lunchtime. Open Monday–Saturday 12pm to 4pm; Saturday 7:30pm to 10pm. Bio & Cie, Restauration Biologique, 12 rue Alberti, Nice, Tel: 04 93 01 94 70; Web site: www.bio-et-cie.com.

Other Regions

See the regional *bio* food organization Web sites listed under Health Food Stores, some of which include listings for restaurants. Many health food stores and markets serve prepared foods and wonderful picnic supplies.

You will find a free online guidebook to all vegetarian and organic restaurants in France at www.laplage.fr/guidebio/index.html. Click on the map to locate restaurants by region and town.

SPECIAL DIETS

The French phrase for "gluten-free" is *sans gluten*. Gluten-free foods can be found in many of the health food and grocery stores listed here. Look for the brands Valpiform, Nature et Compagnie, Schär, and Glutano. Schär makes gluten-free baguettes and other sandwich breads that are available in health food stores. If you are highly sensitive and or have celiac disease, be aware that flour is used in many dishes in France. Ask before you eat sauces, patés, sausages, meat mixes, and, more obviously, salad croutons.

The French Association for Gluten Intolerance can be found at www. afdiag.org. The site is in French.

For people with cow dairy allergies, France has a bounty of goat (chèvre) and sheep (brebis) milk products, often, though not always, tolerated by those who cannot consume cow dairy. If you cannot consume cow dairy products, read labels carefully, as sometimes cheeses are made with a combination of milks. The word *vache* means "cow" in French, so if you see the words *lait du vache* on a label, avoid the cheese. Some of the most amazing cheeses are made with goat and sheep milk. Banon cheese, so called because it is traditionally made in and around the Provence town of Banon, is divine—it is like brie, only creamier. Specially made from raw goat milk, it is wrapped in chestnut leaves and tied with raffia.

For a treat, try brousse, a fresh and creamy cheese made from either sheep or goat milk and often served with honey. The Gouiran Family has been breeding Le Rove goats since 1480! And one of their specialties is brousse made from the milk of their own goats. Open daily February to October 8am to 12:30pm, 5pm to 8pm. The Gouiran Family, 17 rue Adrien-Isnardon, Le Rove, Provence; Tel: 04 91 09 92 33.

Other French cheeses to look for include Ossau-Iraty, made from sheep milk in the French Pyrénées; Chabichou du Poitou, a soft goat cheese from south of the Loire Valley; and Crottin de Chavignol, another goat cheese from the Loire Valley.

Aux Biscuits D'Antoine makes organic and gluten-free biscuits with buckwheat. Aux Biscuits D'Antoine, 5 Petite rue, Etivey; Tel: 03 86 55 71 73; E-mail: contact@biscuits-antoine.com; Web site: www. biscuits-antoine.com.

Helpful French Words for Those with Special Diet Concerns

Egg-free = *Sans œuf*	Soy-free = *Sans soja*
Milk-free = *Sans lait*	Wheat-free = *Sans blé*
Peanut-free = *Sans arachide*	

Sarl Jean Herve makes lacto-fermented grains, seeds, and nut and fruit pastes. Sarl Jean Herve, rue de la République, Clion, Indre; Tel: 02 54 38 66 03; Fax: 02 54 38 66 04; E-mail: jean@herve-sarl.fr; Web site: www.herve-sarl.fr.

Recreation
HIKING

Walking and hiking are popular sports and leisure activities in France, and trails are abundant throughout the country. Long-distance trails are designated in red with the abbreviation GR, from *sentier de grand randonée,* which means long-distance footpath. Short-distance trails, or *petite randonée,* are marked in yellow with the letters PR.

Open Monday–Friday 10am to 6pm, the Fédération Française de la Randonnée Pédestre (The French Federation of Hiking) also has a very useful Web site, located at www.ffrandonnee.fr and available only in French, which offers good information about walking routes all over France. Click on "Itinéraires" and "700 idées randos," followed by "entrez." Search the map by region or by drop-down menu for desired area, length of walk (see "La durée"), terrain (see "Le milieu"), and season (see "La saison"). Easy-to-use general maps of the GRs (long-distance trails) and lists of accommodations along each route can be found at www.gr-infos.com. Fédération Française de la Randonnée Pédestre, 64 rue du Dessous des Berges, 75013, Paris; Métro: 14 Bibliothèque François Mitterrand; Tel: 01 44 89 93 93; Fax: 01 40 35 85 67.

Based in Strasbourg, The Club Vosgien focuses on the northeastern Alsatian area of France, promoting hiking, route maintenance, and the training of hiking guides. Detailed maps are available for about 11 euros each. For more information, go to www.club-vosgien.com.

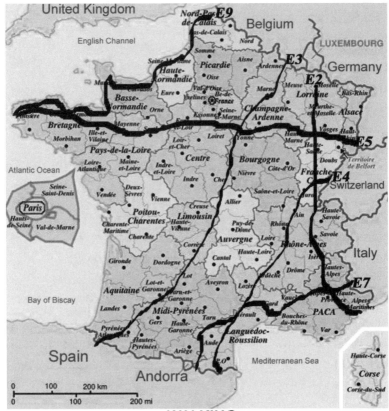

WALKING

Approximate French Part of
European Walking Routes
E2 E3 E4 E5 E7 E9
See www.eva-ewv-ferp.com
for details about the routes

Walking guidebooks and hiking maps of France can be purchased from www.francewalkingtours.com, which carries the largest selection of European and U.S. maps and books about hiking in France. You can also find maps and books at the Institut Geographique National Web site www.ign.fr, which also offers a guide for the randonnée.

On the western Provence Mediterranean coast, you can walk ten miles along a seawall *(digue),* which is closed to cars between

Saintes-Maries-de-la-Mer and Salin de Giraud, and pass beautiful grey sand dunes and seabirds. Access the downloadable La Digue à la Mer brochure at www.tourisme.ville-arles.fr/document/pdfs_document/1119376497.pdf for route information, .

There are a number of routes to Santiago de Compostela, Spain, that run through France. For more information see Sacred Sites. There are also numerous other hiking possibilities listed in the City and Regional Highlights and Wild and Natural Resources sections. See the *Green Earth Guide* Map of Euro-Walking Routes on page 52.

BIKING

Biking *(vélo)* is a wonderful recreational activity, and many people enjoy the multiple bike routes that run through France. Like hiking, biking can also be a practical transportation choice (see Bike Rental in the Getting Around section), and every train station has parking areas where you will find rows of bicycles. For biking routes through France, go to www.ecf.com, the site for the European Cyclists Federation (ECF), which lists routes all over Europe on the Euro Cycle Network or EuroVelo. One of the most popular routes is EuroVelo #6. The route is so popular it has its own Web site, which can be found at www.eurovelo6.org. EuroVelo #6 runs from the French Atlantic coast to the Romanian Black Sea coast, and you can bike stages of the route or the entire thing. The ECF Web site offers downloadable reports that detail the twelve different EuroVelo routes. See the *Green Earth Guide* Map Velo 6, on page 54.

You can explore the bike routes on the Brittany Green Trails at www.randobreizh.org/VeloroutesVoiesVertesBretagne_index.php.

There are numerous biking paths in the Camargue nature preserve (see Natural Resources). Go to www.tourisme.ville-arles.fr/us/a8/a8c.php for nine downloadable brochures with routes and information.

In Provence, the Luberon mountain range contains over 236 kilometers of marked cycling routes. For maps with routes, accommodations, and sites, visit www.veloloisirluberon.com.

There are countless biking and hiking routes through La Forêt des Landes (Landes Forest National Park) in the Aquitaine region. See more information under Bordeaux in City and Regional Highlights.

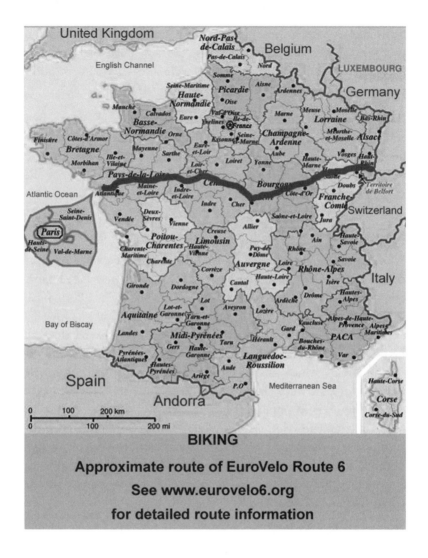

BIKING

Approximate route of EuroVelo Route 6

See www.eurovelo6.org

for detailed route information

The Tour de France is held the last three weeks in July. Go to www. letour.fr for full route and date information.

Cycling in France, from the Ulysses Guides, is a good reference book. For more information, go to www.ulyssesguides.com. There are also numerous other biking possibilities listed in the Regional Highlights and Wild and Natural Resources sections.

YOGA

Yoga means union—the integration of body, mind, and spirit. It involves both gentle and strenuous stretching exercises, meditation,

The Spirit of Yoga, by Kathy Phillips. Barrons Educational Series, 2006.

Yoga: Mastering the Secrets of Matter and the Universe, by Alain Daniélou. Inner Traditions, 1991.

Yoga Journal magazine. Visit www.yogajournal.com.

and breathing techniques to help calm the mind and strengthen the body. There are over forty different types of yoga, some of the most common include Iyengar, a gentle, classic style using props; Ashtanga, also called power yoga, which moves more quickly from pose to pose; Bikram, or hot yoga, which is done in a room heated to around 100°F, which makes for an intense workout; and Hatha yoga, a gentle, relaxing, and meditative form. Kripalu, Kundalini, and Sivananda are other common yoga types.

As you might imagine, yoga centers are plentiful throughout France. A sampling of yoga centers in Paris and Avignon is listed below. Two online directories, www.yoga-centers-directory.net/france.htm and www.yogafinder.com/yogacity.cfm?yogacountry=France, allow you to search for and locate yoga classes all over France.

Paris
Centre de Yoga du Marais, 72 rue du Vertbois, 75003, Paris; Tel: 01 42 74 24 92; E-mail: yogamarais@wanadoo.fr.

Sivananda Yoga; Tel: 01 40 26 77 49; E-mail: paris@sivananda.org; Web site: www.sivananda.org.

Centre Samasthiti Ashtanga Vinyasa Yoga, 23 rue de la Cerisaie, 75004, Paris; Tel: 01 44 07 31 33; Email: caroline.boulinguez@sa-mathitistudio.net; Web site: www.samasthitistudio.com.

Yoganamaria, 5 rue Trésor, 75004, Paris; Tel 06 64 39 24 73; Email: ashtanga@yoganamaria.com; Web site: www.yoganamaria.com.

Le Yoga Bikram Paris has two locations with walk-in classes taught in both French and English. Le Yoga Bikram, 17 rue du Faubourg,

75009, Montmartre; Door Code: A4246; Tel: 01 42 47 18 52. Le Bikram Yoga location, 13 rue Simon Le Franc, 75004, Paris; Web site: www.bikramyogaparis.com.

Avignon

In Avignon, visit Relax Atelier, which offers yoga and sophrologie. Relax Atelier; Tel: 04 90 85 93 31; E-mail: relaxatelier@orange.fr.

Centre de Yoga Iyengar is open Wednesdays with classes at 12:30 and 6:30pm. Centre de Yoga Iyengar, 50 rue des Lices, Avignon; Tel: 04 66 64 56 63.

Centre Atma offers Hatha yoga classes and Ayurvedic massage. Centre Atma, 50 rue des Lices, Avignon.

MEDITATION

There are numerous opportunities for meditation practice in France, and the following suggestions are only a few of the many options.

Thich Nhat Hanh is a Vietnamese Zen monk known for his inspiring and thoughtful books, peace advocacy, and humanitarian work. He has written many books, including *Being Peace, The Sun My Heart,* and *Peace Is Every Step.* Thich Nhat Hanh's retreat center, Plum Village, is located in southwestern France. Four hamlets (Thenac, Dieulivol, Loubès-Bernac, Puyguilhem) comprise the Plum Village community; there are two for men and couples, and another two for women and couples. Your visits can run from one to three weeks, and there are special retreats held throughout the year. Arrangements must be made in advance at www.plumvillage.org.

Dashang Kagyu Ling Temple des Mille Bouddhas (Temple of One Thousand Buddhas) hosts its Sacred Dance Festival every August. Open weekdays 2pm to 5pm and weekends 2:30pm to 6pm; July–August 10am to noon, 2pm to 6:45pm. Admission is 4 euros. Dashang Kagyu Ling Temple des Mille Bouddhas, Château de Plaige, 71320, La Boulaye; Tel: 03 85 79 62 52 or 03 85 79 62 53; E-mail: dashang. kagyu.ling@wanadoo.fr; Web site: www.mille-bouddhas.com.

Centre Vipassana France—Dhamma Mahi, Le Bois Plante, Louesme, 89350, Champignelles; Tel: 386 45 75 14; E-mail: info@mahi. dhamma.org; Web site: www.mahi.dhamma.org.

Centre d'études tibétaines, Montchardon, 38160, Izeron; Tel: 04 76 38 33 13; Web site: www.montchardon.org.

Centre de méditation Shambhala de Marseille, 55 rue Jaubert, Marseille; Tel: 04 91 33 08 73 or 04 91 26 61 87; E-mail: marseille@shambhala.fr; Web site: marseille.shambhala.fr.

Centre Shambhala de Paris, 23 rue Titon, Paris; Tel: 01 43 73 65 77; E-mail: paris@shambhala.fr; Web site: www.paris.shambhala.fr.

Dechen Chöling, Le Mas Marvent, Saint-Yrieix-sous-Aixe, Limoges; Tel: 05 55 03 55 52; E-mail: programmes@dechencholing.org; Web site: www.dechencholing.org/english.

Visit Librairie Holstein, a French-language bookstore specializing in Buddhist philosophy. Librairie Holstein, 55 rue des Fourbisseurs, Avignon.

Bouddhisme Actualités, a French Buddhism magazine, can be explored at www.bouddhisme-actu.net.

The Web site for events and classes in Toulouse, Montpellier, Nîmes, and other cities can be found at www.bouddhismetoulouse.org.

THERMAL BATHS

France has more than one hundred natural mineral and thermal springs that have been used as therapeutic healing centers for centuries. They are commonly referred to as baths, or *bains* in French. Many spa towns have as part of their name the word *bains,* which you will notice in the listings below. Don't be confused if you see more than one spa listed for a thermal spring, as some of the towns with thermal springs have multiple establishments making use of the naturally hot water.

Today the springs provide a multigenerational recreational and luxury activity, but they are still considered therapeutic. The French national health system covers some of the treatment costs for French citizens. In France, different mineral springs are known for addressing different ailments. See the *Green Earth Guide* Map to Baths and Spas in France on page 58.

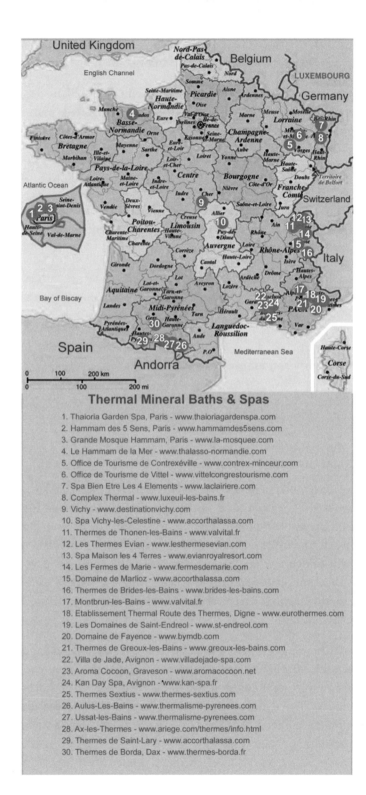

Thermal Mineral Baths & Spas

1. Thaioria Garden Spa, Paris - www.thaioriagardenspa.com
2. Hammam des 5 Sens, Paris - www.hammamdes5sens.com
3. Grande Mosque Hammam, Paris - www.la-mosquee.com
4. Le Hammam de la Mer - www.thalasso-normandie.com
5. Office de Tourisme de Contrexéville - www.contrex-minceur.com
6. Office de Tourisme de Vittel - www.vittelcongrestourisme.com
7. Spa Bien Etre Les 4 Elements - www.laclairiere.com
8. Complex Thermal - www.luxeuil-les-bains.fr
9. Vichy - www.destinationvichy.com
10. Spa Vichy-les-Celestine - www.accorthalassa.com
11. Thermes de Thonen-les-Bains - www.valvital.fr
12. Les Thermes Evian - www.lesthermesevian.com
13. Spa Maison les 4 Terres - www.evianroyalresort.com
14. Les Fermes de Marie - www.fermesdemarie.com
15. Domaine de Marlioz - www.accorthalassa.com
16. Thermes de Brides-les-Bains - www.brides-les-bains.com
17. Montbrun-les-Bains - www.valvital.fr
18. Etablissement Thermal Route des Thermes, Digne - www.eurothermes.com
19. Les Domaines de Saint-Endreol - www.st-endreol.com
20. Domaine de Fayence - www.bymdb.com
21. Thermes de Greoux-les-Bains - www.greoux-les-bains.com
22. Villa de Jade, Avignon - www.villadejade-spa.com
23. Aroma Cocoon, Graveson - www.aromacocoon.net
24. Kan Day Spa, Avignon - www.kan-spa.fr
25. Thermes Sextius - www.thermes-sextius.com
26. Aulus-Les-Bains - www.thermalisme-pyrenees.com
27. Ussat-les-Bains - www.thermalisme-pyrenees.com
28. Ax-les-Thermes - www.ariege.com/thermes/info.html
29. Thermes de Saint-Lary - www.accorthalassa.com
30. Thermes de Borda, Dax - www.thermes-borda.fr

Vichy, at the rim of the Massif Central, is a famous spa town. Go to www.destinationvichy.com/eaux/sources.htm for the locations of the prized Vichy water. There are three hotels specializing in thermal water treatments: Les Celestins, les Domes, and Callou. Information about all three is available at www.destinationvichy.com.

Montbrun-les-Bains is located eleven kilometers from Sault. For more reasons to visit Sault, see Aroma. Montbrun-les-Bains, Station thermale, 26570, Montbrun Les Bains; Tel: 04 75 28 80 75; E-mail: montbrun@valvital.fr.

Les Thermes Evian—the well-known Evian thermal springs and baths—is located on Lake Leman, as the French call it. In Switzerland, however, it is known as Lake Geneva. Les Bains Evian offers spa treatments a la carte or in package deals. Les Thermes Evian, Place de la Liberation BP 8, Evian-les-Bains; Tel: 04 50 75 02 30; Web site: www.lesthermesevian.com/indexgb.php.

Thermes de Thonon-les-Bains offers mineral baths with spa and therapeutic treatments. Thermes de Thonon-les-Bains, boulevard de la Corniche, Thonon-les-Bains; Tel: 05 50 26 17 22; E-mail: thonon@valvital.fr; Web site: www.valvital.fr.

There are three thermal spas in the very southern region of France in Ariège Pyrénées. Les Thermes d'Aulus specializes in metabolic illnesses and urinary tract issues. Les Thermes d'Aulus, Aulus-les-Bains, 09140, Ariège, Midi-Pyrénées; Tel: 05 61 96 01 46; E-mail: contact@thermalisme-pyrenees.com; Web site: www.ariege.com/thermes-aulus/info.html and www.thermalisme-pyrenees.com.

Ussat-les-Bains specializes in ailments resulting from stress and anxiety, including migraines. Ussat-les-Bains, Domaine Thermal d'Ussat-les-Bains, Avenue des Thermes, 09400, Ussat-Les-Bains; Tel: 05 61 02 20 03; E-mail: thermes.ussat@wanadoo.fr; Web site: perso.orange.fr/thermes.ussat.

And finally, Ax-les-Thermes specializes in rheumatic illnesses, as well as ear, nose, and throat ailments. For more information, go to www.ariège.com/thermes/info.html.

Dax is a spa town in southern France, west of Toulouse, known for its hot springs. It is accessible from Paris by the TGV high-speed train. The Thermes de Borda specializes in treatments for rheumatologic diseases. You can visit the hot baths for day use and pay an hourly rate or go for the six- to twenty-one-day intensive therapy sessions. In addition to the thermal water, the Thermes de Borda employs pelotherapy, using the local Dax peloid mud from the river. You can find hourly rate information hiding under "Leisure" on the Web page. Thermes de Borda, 30 rue des Lazaristes, Dax; Tel: 05 58 74 86 13; Web site: www.thermes-borda.fr.

Thermes de Gréoux-les-Bains is located in the natural regional park of Verdon, which includes 150 kilometers of marked walking trails. Thermes de Gréoux-les-Bains, Chaîne Thermale du Soleil, 5 Avenue des Marronniers, 04800, Gréoux-les-Bains; Tel: 04 92 70 40 00; Office Municipal de Tourisme Tel: 04 92 78 01 08; E-mail: tourisme@greoux-les-bains.com; Web site: www.greoux-les-bains.com.

EuroThermes operates nine thermal spring spas around France, including one in Digne-les-Bains, Provence. Les Thermes de Digne, BP 163, 04005, Digne les Bains; Tel: 04 92 32 32 92; E-mail: thermes_digne@wanadoo.fr; Web site: www.eurothermes.com.

In the Alsace region, the Complex Thermal specializes in treatments for rheumatic and gynecologic ailments. Open March 3–November 8. Complex Thermal, 3 rue des Thermes, Luxeuil-les-Bains; Tel: 03 84 40 44 22; Web site: www.luxeuil-les-bains.fr.

In Paris, a Turkish hammam (bath house) can be found at the Grand Mosque. The Hammam is open for women on Monday, Wednesday, Thursday, and Saturday 10am to 9pm, and on Friday 2pm to 9pm. For men, it is open on Tuesday 2pm to 9pm, and on Sunday 10am to 9pm. Package deals that include massages and scrubs start from about 38 euros. Bring your own towels or pay the extra charge. Save time for tea in the not-to-be-missed Salon de Thé (see more details under Food). La Mosquée, 39 rue Geoffroy Saint-Hilaire, Paris; Tel: 43 31 38 14; Web site www.la-mosquee.com.

At the Chaine Thermale du Soleil Web site you can explore twenty thermal stations. For more details, go to www.chainethermale.fr.

OUTDOOR FILM AND THEATER

In the summer, outdoor movie screenings are held in La Villette, the largest park in Paris. Entry is free for viewing movies, so bring a picnic and enjoy. Chair rentals cost 6.50 euros. For more information, go to www.cinema.arbo.com.

The Avignon Theater Festival is held annually for three weeks in July. Theater companies from around Europe perform in both indoor and outdoor venues. Be prepared for late, late nights, and book your accommodations far in advance. For more information, go to www.festival-avignon.com. There is ample street entertainment in Avignon, including the Fringe Festival, also known as Festival OFF. For more information, go to www.avignonoff.net.

Health

If you want to maintain a treatment plan, explore modalities in a foreign country, or seek out new experiences, you can make use of the following resources to help you find health practitioners and services in the regions you are visiting.

France has a long history of using natural remedies for health care. Many therapies considered alternative are actually practiced by medical doctors, and in some cases only medical doctors are allowed to practice these modalities. In France, the medical attributes of aromatherapy are taken seriously and are highly regarded, and some medical doctors are specially trained in the therapeutic use of essential oils. In some cases, non-medical doctors cannot even be trained in aromatherapy. For more information, see the Aroma section below.

ANTHROPOSOPHICAL MEDICINE

Based on the use of natural rhythms and remedies, anthroposophical medicine was developed by the scientist and philosopher Rudolf Steiner. Anthroposophy comes from two Greek words: "Anthropos," which means "human being," and "sophia," which means "wisdom." Anthroposophy can be translated as "human wisdom."

Dr. Rudolf Steiner (1861–1925), a scientist and artist, developed anthroposophical medicine in 1913 based on his studies of natural, social, and spiritual realms, from which he concluded that plants, animals, humans, the earth, and the cosmos are all living things with vital forces. Greatly influenced by the German philosopher Johann Wolfgang Goethe (1749–1832), Steiner developed not just theories

While the raw plant and berries of mistletoe are poisonous, they are safe and even medicinal as specially prepared extracts. In Europe, mistletoe extracts are used as immune stimulants and cancer therapies. Mistletoe is a semi-parasitic plant that grows on a variety of trees, including oak, pine, and apple. Traveling through France you will see a profusion of mistletoe in the trees. In Europe, a common mistletoe remedy is manufactured by the Weleda company under the name of Iscador, and has been used for over eighty years. For more information, see their Web site at www.iscador.com. Currently, mistletoe extract is not legal in the United States, except for use in clinical trials conducted by the National Center for Complementary and Alternative Medicine (NCCAM). For more information, go to www.nccam.nih.gov/health/eurmistletoe. See plate 15.

and systems of health, but also systems of education (Waldorf schools), agriculture (biodynamic farming), astronomy, color, and movement (eurythmy).

Dr. Rudolf Hauschka (1891–1969), an Austrian chemist, worked with Rudolf Steiner to develop remedies using anthroposophical theories, an understanding of plants, minerals, and metals, and their interactions and effects on human health and vitality.

Based on in-depth studies of rhythm and a combination of homeopathic potentiation and rhythmic exposure to elemental polarities, Dr. Hauschka, along with Dr. Ita Wegman, another Steiner associate, developed what were to become the WALA (Warmth/Ash, Light/Ash) remedies. The plant-based remedies are made from wild or biodynamically grown plants.

Dr. Hauschka collaborated with Elisabeth Sigmund (1924–), a cosmetologist, and together they cofounded Dr. Hauschka Skin Care Products.

To contact the French Association for Anthroposophical Patients (Association de Patients de la Médecine d'orientation Anthroposophique, or APMA), call 03 25 40 88 95 or 06 77 08 28 47.

Spiritual Science and the Art of Healing, by Victor Bott. Healing Arts Press, 1996.

The Fourfold Path to Healing, by Thomas S. Cowan, MD, with Sally Fallon and Jaimen McMillan. New Trends Publishing, 2004. Combines anthroposophical medicine with the Dr. Weston Price diet.

Physicians Association for Anthroposophical Medicine provides a list of anthroposophical resources at www.paam.net and www. artemisia.net.

MASSAGE

Therapeutic massage usually involves a full-body massage with or without oil. While there are different techniques, the general purpose is to relieve muscle tension, increase circulation, and foster relaxation. Bodywork is a broad term covering many different techniques of physical touch and manipulation. Popular in Europe, reflexology is a type of massage based on the reflex zones of the feet and their correlation to the whole body.

A word on modesty and the French: Forget about it. Many European countries, France included, have a different view of the body. Often your massage therapist will not leave the room while you disrobe, or will leave but expects you to emerge for your massage in nothing but a disposable thong—no sheet or towel will be forthcoming.

Many clinics, spas, and thermal baths offer a variety of massage services. The following resources include only a few of many massage and bodywork options.

For therapeutic foot and hand massages, referred to as reflexology, see the Web site for the Federation Francaise de Reflexologues (Federation of French Reflexologists) at www.reflexologues.fr. Go to "annuaire" and click on the map for regional lists of reflexology practitioners.

The Hammam at the Grand Mosque in Paris offers a succession of steam baths with package deals, including massages and scrubs, starting from about 38 euros. The Hammam is open for women Monday, Wednesday, Thursday, and Saturday 10am to 9pm, and Friday 2pm to 9pm. For men, it is open Tuesday 2pm to 9pm, Sunday 10am to 9pm. La Mosquée, 39 rue Geoffroy Saint-Hilaire, Paris; Tel: 43 31 38 14; Web site: www.la-mosquee.com.

OSTEOPATHY

Osteopathic doctors focus on the musculoskeletal system. Craniosacral therapies developed from the field of osteopathy, and osteopathy and chiropractic share some theories and techniques. To find an osteopath near where you are staying, go to the Web site for the Chambre Nationale des Ostéopathes or National House of Osteopaths. Chambre Nationale des Ostéopathes, 118 rue Lauriston, 75016, Paris; E-mail: cnosteo@cnosteo.com; Web site: www.cnosteo.com.

NATUROPATHY

Naturopathic medicine treats health conditions by utilizing the body's inherent ability to heal. It involves a variety of therapies, including diet, herbs, homeopathy, and hydrotherapy. There are six basic principles to naturopathic medicine: to work with the healing power of nature; to treat the cause rather than the effect; to do no harm; to treat the whole person; to have the physician be a teacher; and to understand that prevention is the best cure.

In France, *naturothérapie* (naturopathy) is practiced by *naturothérapeutes* who have completed a three-year university master's degree in naturotherapie medicine after a doctorate in medicine (human, veterinary, dentistry, or pharmacy). Association Nationale de Naturothéropeutes (A2N) Domus Medica, 79 rue de Tocqueville, 75017, Paris.

The *naturothérapie* degree, known as the DUMENAT (Master of Natural Medicines), is taught at the Faculty of Medicine of Bobigny. This degree was created in 1982 at the University Paris XIII in order that medical doctors could be trained extensively in natural modalities. The DUMENAT covers seven disciplines: homeopathy, phytotherapy, acupuncture, mesotherapy, osteopathy, auriculotherapy, and naturothérapie. Faculty of Medicine of Bobigny, 74 rue Mar-

Combining Old and New: Naturopathy for the 21st Century, by Robert Thiel. Whitman Publishing, 2001.

The American Association of Naturopathic Physicians can be found online at www.naturopathic.org.

cel Cachin, 93017, Bobigny; Métro: Line 7 La Courneuve; Tel: 01 48 38 76 11.

HOMEOPATHY

Homeopathy is a specific healing system in which minute doses of specially prepared natural remedies are used to trigger a healing response in an individual. A homeopath prescribes a remedy based on the pattern of symptoms with which a person presents. Homeopathic remedies can be used for a wide range of conditions, from acute illness and injury to complicated chronic conditions.

Developed over two hundred years ago by the German physician Samuel Hahnemann, homeopathy remains in wide use throughout the world. There are two key homeopathic concepts: the Law of Potentiation, which states that medicine can be stronger or more effective when more diluted; and the Law of Similars, which holds that like cures like.

To locate homeopathic doctors while you are in France, go to the Web site for the French Homeopathic Medicine National Association and click on "annuaire homeopaths" for the map of area practitioners. French Homeopathic Medicine National Association (Syndicat National des Médecins Homeopathes Français), 79 rue de Tocqueville, 75017, Paris; Tel: 01 44 29 01 31; Web site: www.snmhf.org.

TIP Hahnemann's Grave

You can find Samuel Hahnemann's grave in Division 19 at the Père Lachaise Cemetery in Paris (see more information under **City and Regional Highlights**).

> *The Homeopathic Revolution: Why Famous People and Cultural Heroes Choose Homeopathy,* by Dana Ullman, MPH. North Atlantic Books, 2007.
>
> *Everybody's Guide to Homeopathic Medicines, Third revised edition,* by Stephen Cummings, MD, and Dana Ullman, MPH. Tarcher, 2004.
>
> Homeopathic Educational Services can be found at www.homeopathic.com.

Homeopathy is very popular in France. One of the largest homeopathic manufacturers in the world, Boiron was founded in France in the early 1900s. The world headquarters of Laboratoires Boiron are still in Sainte-Foy-les-Lyon. Most drugstores in France sell homeopathic remedies and some pharmacies specialize in homeopathy. Below you will find contact information for three homeopathic pharmacies *(pharmacie homéopathique)* in Paris.

Pharmacie Homéopathique Weber is near the place Vendôme and has English-speaking practitioners. Pharmacie Homéopathique Weber, 8 rue des Capucines; Métro: Opera/Auber; Tel: 01 42 61 03 07.

Pharmacie Homéopathique Lahyani, 83 Avenue Ledru, Rollin; Tel: 01 43 47 31 30.

Pharmacie Homéopathique Maubeuge, 58 rue Maubeuge, Paris; Tel: 01 48 78 54 69.

AYURVEDIC MEDICINE

Ayurveda means "the science of life." A comprehensive medical system that originated in ancient India, Ayurveda is one of the oldest medical systems in the world, dating back thousands of years. It has common themes with Chinese medicine systems, including working with the life force energy (called "prana" in Ayurveda, "Chi" or "Qi" in Chinese). Ayurveda works with doshas—different body and personality temperaments—which are similar to more modern metabolic and blood-typing systems.

Ayurveda: The Science of Self-Healing, by Vasant Lad. Lotus Press, 2002.

Ayurveda: Life, Health and Longevity, by Dr. Robert Svoboda. Penguin Books, 1993.

Radical Healing, by Rudolph Ballentine, MD. Crown Books, 1999.

Ayurvedic medicine incorporates all five senses—touch, sound, color, aroma, and taste—into therapies, and treatments involve a combination of diet, herbs, aromatherapy, bodywork, exercise, and spiritual practice. Yoga is the movement and spirit element of Ayurvedic medicine (see more information under **Yoga**).

To find Ayurvedic practitioners while you are in France, go to the Ayurvedic Professional Association at www.ayurveda-france.org. Click on "Les professionals," where you will find a map that lists area practitioners.

ACUPUNCTURE AND TRADITIONAL CHINESE MEDICINE

Traditional Chinese medicine is a four-thousand-year-old system of health based more on energy than biochemistry. It has common themes with Ayurvedic medicine, including working with Qi (or Chi), the vital life force energy. Therapies include herbs, acupuncture, bodywork, exercise, diet, and lifestyle. Assessments include pulse readings, tongue diagnosis, acupuncture point palpation, and health history. The key elements include the interrelationship of all systems and organs of the body, balance within the polarities of yin and yang, as well as the integration of body, mind, and spirit. The eight guiding principles in Chinese medicine include external/internal, cold/heat, excess/deficiency, and yin/yang.

Acupuncture is a healing art that has been used in China for thousands of years. Acupuncturists work with the Chi (or Qi) energy, which flows through specific pathways in the body called meridians. These meridians form an energetic network that traverses the entire body and joins together all of its organ systems. Along each meridian's course, near the surface of the body, are points at which the Qi is most accessible for stimulation. To stimulate these points, thin, sterile needles are inserted at specific points determined by the acupuncturist's examination and diagnosis. The purpose of acupuncture is to move and balance the Qi, thus restoring health and harmony in the body.

Research funded by the National Institute of Health at the University of Vermont is demonstrating the physiological mechanisms of acupuncture. Findings show that acupuncture stretches connective tissue, creating a cell response that leads to changes in brain chemistry.

In France, only medical doctors can legally make diagnoses and use acupuncture, but there is a tolerance of TCM practitioners who are not MDs. The National Federation of Traditional Chinese Medicine (Fédération Nationale de Médecine Traditionnelle Chinoise, or FN-MTC), 7 rue Louis Prével, 06000, Nice; Tel: 08 70 30 48 70; E-mail: contact@fnmtc.fr; Web site: www.fnmtc.fr. Click on "annuaire des practiciers" to find practioners by region.

AROMATHERAPY

For information about aromatherapy, please see the Aroma and Especially Lavender sections.

HERBS AND REMEDIES

I find irresistible shops filled with bags, bottles, shelves, and drawers of dried herbs, tinctures, ointments, and oils. There are a number of medicinal herb stores *(herboristeries)* in Paris. I have included here some of my favorites.

In this small but wonderful true medicinal herb store, Herboristerie d'Hipocrates, there are over nine hundred medicinal plants and remedies sold by the ounce in a simple paper bag or glass package. Herboristerie d'Hipocrates, 42 rue Saint-Andre-des-Arts, Paris. ☛ green earth guide favorite.

In operation since 1927, Herboristerie de Montparnasse is filled with medicinal herbs, and it is good spot for travelers feeling under the weather. Herboristerie Montparnasse, 38 rue Montparnasse, Paris; Tel: 01 45 48 34 81.

Herboristerie de la place de Clichy, 87 rue Amsterdam, Airs; Tel: 01 48 74 83 32; Web site: www.pharma-concept-fr.biz.

Natural Health Product Stores

Fleurs Essences et Harmonie sells flower essences and other natural products online and has three stores in Paris at the following locations: 53 rue des Batignolles, 73 bis, avenue de Wagram, and 11 boulevard Port Royal. For more information, go to www.lesfleursde-bach.com.

Guayapi sells organic teas and health products. Guayapi, 73 rue de Charenton, Paris; Tel: 01 43 46 14 69; Web site: www.guayapi.com.

The Lehning Laboratoires is located in a rural area 10 kilometers northeast of Metz. They manufacture homeopathic remedies, herbs, and natural care products. The Lehning Laboratoires, 3 rue du Petit Marais, 57640, Sainte-Barb; Web site: www.lehning.com.

Heliopole offers a nice selection of flower essences. Heliopole, 34–36 rue de Enclos, Moyenmoutier; Tel: 03 29 63 37 54; E-mail: heliopolefrance@aol.com; Web site: www.heliopole.com.

Phytofrance is a laboratory near Montpellier that produces aromatherapy, phytotherapy, natural cosmetics, and homeopathy remedies with organic herbs. Phytofrance, Complexe la Gastade, BP5, Candillargues; Tel: 04 67 29 64 25; E-mail: phytofrance@wanadoo.fr; Web site: www.phytofrance.com.

Institut Méditerranéen de Documentation d'Enseignement et de Recherche sur les Plantes Médicinales (IMDERPLAM) conducts courses and research on plant medicines, including herbs, phyto-therapy, homeopathy, Chinese medicine, aromatherapy, and nutri-tional therapy. Most courses are long-term commitments, lasting two to three years; however, some shorter workshops and confer-ence-style classes are available. Institut Méditerranéen de Documen-tation d'Enseignement et de Recherche sur les Plantes Médicinales (IMDERPLAM), Mas des Bonnes Ouest RD 106, 34130, Candill-argues; Tel: 04 67 29 60 05; Web site: www.imderplam.com.

CLINICS AND SPAS

In France, the water cures are taken seriously, and many of the ther-mal baths *(bains)* have medical and professional staff offering treat-ments for various ailments, in addition to providing more common spa therapies. For a short list of the many thermal baths around France, see more information under Recreation and also City and Re-gional Highlights. Spa-goers take note: Remember what I said about modesty and the French? Well, this applies to spas and clinic as well. See the *Green Earth Guide* Map to Baths and Spas in France, page 58.

Thalassotherapy is the term used for treatments using sea water (from the Greek *thalassa*). There are twenty-six thalassotherapy spas and clinics lining France's coast. "Water and Fitness in France," a bro-chure offered by the France Government Tourist Office Web site, lists all the thalassotherapy centers that dot the coastline of France, as well as other spa and water treatment facilities. Go to us.franceguide.com/what-to-do/wellbeing/home.html?NodeID=143 and click on "Download Brochure," where you will find a forty-page full-color brochure about spa and water therapies throughout France.

See the *Green Earth Guide* Map to Thalassotherapy Centers in France, page 71.

Paris
Thaioria Garden Spa offers a range of spa therapies and specializes in Thai massage bodywork, with prices ranging from 45 to 150 eu-ros. Open every day from 11am to 8:30pm. Thaioria Garden Spa, 3–5 rue Desaix, Paris; Métro: Duplex; Tel: 01 56 58 21 03; Web site: www.thaioriagardenspa.com.

At Hammam Les 5 Sens, prices start from 20 euros for the ham-mam (steam bath). Other spa therapies, such as massage and scrubs

offers classic and Ayurvedic massage therapy. Le Hammam de la Mer, 2 rue Guynemer, Luc-sur-Mer; Tel: 02 31 97 32 22; E-mail: accueil@thalasso-normandie.com; Web site: www.thalasso-normandie.com.

Shopping
NATURAL, UNTREATED, AND ORGANIC

If you happen to be in Paris during the month of October, you can attend the Ethical Fashion Show, where over one hundred companies exhibit and showcase ethical clothing and goods, including organic textiles and free-trade goods. Ethical Fashion Show/Universal Love, 4 rue Trousseau, 75011, Paris: Tel: 01 43 48 94 68; E-mail: contact@ethicalfashionshow.com; Web site: www.ethicalfashion-show.com.

Lea Nature Group manufactures and distributes organic and natural products, including cosmetics, remedies, food, and clothing. Their products are sold throughout France, or you can visit their store. They make particularly adorable baby clothing from organic and fair-trade cotton. Open Monday–Thursday 11am to 7pm, Friday 11am to 6pm. Lea Nature Group, Avenue Paul Langevin, Perigny, La Rochelle; Tel: (0)5 46 34 3000; E-mail: contact@lea-nature.com; Web site: www.lea-nature.com.

Bionat Eco shoes are made in France with vegetable-tanned leather, a process using plant derivatives rather than more hazardous synthetic compounds or metals. The soles of Bionat shoes are made with natural latex from rubber trees instead of plastic. The shoes are available online or at one of their six stores in Longeron, Lyon, Montreuil, Montpellier, Toulouse and Chatenois. See "Magasins" and "Points de Vente" at www.bionat.fr for store locations and hours. Chaussures Bionat, BP 48, 1 rue de l'Industrie, 67730 Chatenois; Tel: (0)3 88 82 5757; Email: info@bionat.fr; Web site: www.bionat.fr.

Ekyog makes original organic and fair-trade cotton clothing for men, women, and babies. They also make bed and bath linens, and they have their own line of yoga wear and organic skin care. Items are available online or at one of their sixteen stores around France, including Montpellier, Nantes, Paris, Quimper, Rennes, and Strasbourg.

For a complete list of stores and more product information, go to www.ekyog.com.

PERSONAL CARE AND NATURAL COSMETICS

The French Professional Association of Ecological and Organic Cosmetics is online at www.cosmebio.org. You can search 140 member companies and nearly four thousand certified products, from eye shadow to toothpaste. French specialties include clays in many colors—traditional green, yellow, and red. Look for lavender everything, including soaps and essential oils. France is also known for its fancy, high-end cosmetics, some of which are now made with an ecological conscience.

One Voice, based in Nantes, offers a guide to cruelty-free cosmetics at www.onevoice-ear.org.

Below you will find only a small selection of the many companies in France manufacturing natural cosmetics and body care products.

Boutique Nature has their own line of natural cosmetics. For more information, go to www.boutique-nature.fr.

Couleur Caramel natural makeup is Ecocert certified and cruelty free. For details, go to www.couleur-caramel.com.

Douces Angevines has a lovely line of *bio* body care and cosmetics. See their Web site at www.lesdoucesangevines.com.

Argiletz specializes in French clay products, including bags and tubes of clay in a rainbow of colors. Look for the numerous other natural brands sold at health food stores, which include Cattier, Melvita, Sanoflore, Florame, Anika, Natessance, Tocophea, and Provence-Argile.

In the university city of Montpellier, there are a few wonderful stores specializing in natural cosmetics, some of which are listed here.

Dolce Natura, a beautiful natural cosmetics and body care store, sells Nelly Grosjean's Vie Arome products (see Aroma), and many other lovely products. Dolce Natura, 15 rue des Soeurs Noires, Montpellier; Tel: 04 67 55 38 97; Web site: www.dolce-natura.com. ☛ green earth guide favorite.

Florame manufactures organic essential oils and diffusers. Not surprisingly, the stores smell divine. The Montpellier store is open Monday 2:30pm to 7pm, and Tuesday–Saturday 10:15am to 1pm, 2:30pm to 7pm. See their Web site for other locations in Paris and Saint-Rémy. Florame, 1 rue du Four des Flammes, near place Saint-Roch, Montpellier; Tel: 04 67 67 90 40; Web site: www.florame. com. ☛ green earth guide favorite.

Melvita, located right next door to the Ekyog *bio* cotton clothing store, is a French manufacturer of body care products, many of which are natural and organic. Be sure and read the labels. Melvita, 25 rue de l'Argenterie, Montpellier; Tel: 04 67 02 07 68; Web site: www.melvita.com.

FAIR TRADE

The International Federation for Alternative Trade defines fair-trade as "a trading partnership based on dialogue, transparency and respect, that seeks greater equity in international trade. It contributes to sustainable development by offering better trading conditions to, and securing the rights of, marginalized producers and workers."

Fair trade is based on fair prices and prompt payment for goods. Fair trade is also based on safe and healthy working environments, and conforms to the United Nations Convention on the Rights of the Child. Fair-trade Web sites include www.fairtrade.org.uk, www. aworldconnected.org, and www.ifat.org.

In France, Max Havelaar is the label to trust when purchasing goods certified as fair trade. Products include coffee, tea, bananas, chocolate, fruit juices, sugar, rice, honey, cotton, spices, and crafts. For more information, go to www.maxhavelaarfrance.org.

Artisans du Monde (Artisans of the World) offers a list of stores and boutiques, by region, which sell fair-trade products. Check out www. artisansdumonde.org. Search under "nos points de vente."

Alter Eco Equitable Commerce is another site that lists fair-trade products and stores by region. For more information, go to www. altereco.com.

Avignon

Artisans du Monde is the Avignon boutique of the organization Artisans du Monde, which sells and promotes fair-trade products from around the world. Open Monday–Saturday 2:30pm to 6:30pm; Wednesday, Friday, and Saturday 10:30am to 12:30pm. Artisans du Monde, 56 rue de la Bonneterie; Tel: 04 90 16 94 54; E-mail: avignon@artisansdumonde.org; Web site: www.artisansdumonde.org.

Maison Alternative et Solidaire (La MAS) is a collective of associations, which includes Greenpeace, Artisans du Monde, and many others. La MAS holds discussion groups and forums, and operates a little fair-trade boutique and bar. Open Tuesday–Saturday 12:30pm to 7pm. Maison Alternative et Solidaire (La MAS), 5 rue des Teinturiers, Avignon; Tel: 04 90 82 59 26; E-mail: maison.altersolidaire@wanadoo.fr.

THRIFT AND SECONDHAND

Thrift or secondhand stores *(une friperie* or *la fripe)* are wonderful places to shop. Often full of clothes, books, art, furniture, kitchen gadgets, and more, they are a treasure trove for travelers interested in recycled items and good prices. Check the hours carefully, as many shops do not keep standard store hours.

In addition, local markets often have lots of options for secondhand goods (see Markets). *Brocantes* are markets for secondhand household items, but you won't usually come across antiques. *Puces* are flea markets. And *vide-greniers,* which means "empty attic," are yard or tag sales.

Eileen Fripe is a tiny, crazy, crammed rummage-style store. Clothes are piled high and spill onto the floor, but the prices are good and shopping is an adventure. Eileen Fripe, 53 rue Monge, Paris.

In Paris, the Village Saint-Paul is hidden behind City Hall, between rue Saint-Paul and rue Saint-Antoine (Métro: Saint-Paul). It is warren of old buildings and courtyards, which are now home to more than sixty secondhand and antique stores, as well as bookstores, galleries, and cafés.

Paris is home to many markets, including the design flea market on Passage du Grande C, and the flea market at place Saint-Sulpice. Many other shopping opportunities are listed under Markets.

Avignon

Insercollect Yoko has a good selection of secondhand clothes at reasonable to cheap prices. Insercollect is in the old part of the city. Open Monday–Friday 9:30am to 12:30pm, 2pm to 6:30pm; Saturday 9:30am to 1pm, 2pm to 6pm. Insercollect Yoko, 1 rue de la Carreterie, Avignon; Tel: 04 90 82 64 11.

There are a few other small secondhand stores in the newer part of Avignon, including Au Royaume de Fatine and Le Relais de Provence. Au Royaume de Fatine, 4 rue des Papalines, Avignon; Tel: 04 90 85 00 27. Le Relais de Provence, ancien chemin du Bac de Ramatuel, Avignon; Tel: 04 90 88 73 86.

MARKETS

Most towns have regular market *(marché)* days, which rotate and alternate by the day of the week, depending on the region. For example, there are markets in some towns on Mondays, and on Tuesdays they are in other towns. Some of the vendors move from village to village, while others stay local. Markets are often held in the central square or a major center of a village, and car traffic is halted in the area. Markets sell a variety of goods, including local meats, charcuterie (cold, cooked meats), fruits, vegetables, cheese, clothes, jewelry, fabrics, shoes, tools, and flowers. Don't miss the many varieties of olives! Weekends are often the big market days, and the earlier you arrive, the better the finds. There are more markets listed under Food and City and Regional Highlights.

Keep your eyes open for *brocantes, puces,* and *vide-greniers.* Antique stores and stalls are more expensive, but treasures abound everywhere. Isle-sur-la-Sorgue, east of Avignon in the Vaucluse area of Provence, is known for its abundance of antique dealers. On Sunday mornings there is a famous market in Isle-sur-la-Sorgue where food, artisan products, *brocante,* and miscellany are sold. See the listing below for more information.

In Paris, there are markets galore. Throughout the twenty arrondissements (districts) there are seventy-eight markets held on varying days of the week. A few historical and classic markets are listed here, and the markets specializing in biologique (organic) foods are listed under the Food section. For a list of all the markets in Paris, compiled by the city of Paris and refined by Clotilde Dusoulier, you can refer to "Markets of Paris" at chocolateandzucchini.com/parismarkets. html.

Paris's oldest and largest market, the Beauvau Marché d'Aligre is open Tuesday–Saturday 8:30am to 1pm. After a three-hour break, selling resumes from 4pm to 7pm. On Sundays the market is only open in the morning from 8:30am to 1pm. Beauvau Marché d'Aligre, rue d'Aligre; Métro: Ledrun Rollin or Bastille; Web site: marchedaligre. free.fr.

One of Paris's oldest covered markets is the Enfants Rouges, which is held Tuesday–Saturday 8:30am to 1pm. After a three-hour break, selling resumes from 4pm to 7pm. The market is open Sunday morning from 8:30am to 1pm. Le Marché des Enfants Rouges, 39 rue de Bretagne in the 3rd arrondissement (3e).

Les Puces is comprised of fourteen markets clustered together around the main street of rue des Rosiers (Métro: Porte de Clingancourt). The markets carry all kinds of goods, including antiques, books, food, clothes, and souvenirs. Open Saturday from 9am to 6pm, Sunday 10am to 6pm, and Monday 11am to 5pm. Maps and more information are available at www.parispuces.com.

In Provence you can find many markets, and a few of the highlights are listed here.

In Riez, an ancient Roman village, the Marché Provençal is held on Wednesday and Saturday mornings. In the summer months there is an evening market on Thursdays from 6pm to midnight, with live music as well as vendors.

Every Saturday morning, all year round, you will find a market in the small city of Apt in Provence. The largest selection of local goods can be found in the summer months. There is also a farmers' market every Tuesday morning in Apt.

In Nice, there are markets every day of the week all year long at place Pierre Gautier in the heart of the old city. Sunday is the food market, and other days you can find books and all manner of secondhand goods. ☛ green earth guide favorite.

Isle-sur-la-Sorgue is beautiful. The old part of the village is surrounded by a little river and the name of the village celebrates this unique feature. The weekly Sunday market is held from 8am to 2pm

bio or *biologique* = organic

le lait = milk

un œuf = egg

le pain = bread

le poulet fermier = free-range chicken

une tranche = a slice

le fromage = cheese

fromage du chèvre or *chèvre* = goat cheese

fromage du Brebis = sheep cheese

miel = honey

huile d'olive = olive oil

sel = salt

vin = wine

huile essentielle = essential oil

Fabriqué en France = Made in France

---

on each side of the river, and you will find connecting bridges every 150 feet or so. Isle-sur-la-Sorgue is known for its year-round antiques, secondhand stores *(brocantes),* and market—and it doesn't disappoint. The goods are of a high quality and at generally fair prices. The market also sells food, artisan products, and clothing. ☞ green earth guide favorite.

In Arles—the land of Van Gogh—there are good markets on Wednesday (at boulevard E. Combes) and Saturday mornings (at boulevard des Lices and boulevard Clémenceau), with some especially fine French rummage at excellent prices. You will also find a variety of ethnic spices and products. ☞ green earth guide favorite.

In the Lorraine region of northeastern France, the village of Metz hosts a large flea and antiques market once or twice monthly, depending on the time of year. It is held in the Centre des Congres, and prices range from fabulous deals to the very expensive. Metz also has a famous Christmas market in the month of December.

BOOKSTORES

Book lovers will think they have died and gone to heaven at www.livre-rare-book.com, which lists rare bookstores all over France and is organized by name of store or by region.

Paris

Shakespeare and Company is a landmark independent bookstore near Notre Dame, with English-language books, author readings, and writing workshops. Open every day 10am to 11pm. Shakespeare and Company, 37 rue de la Bûcherie, Paris; Tel: 1 43 25 40 93; Web site: www.shakespeareco.org.

The Village Voice Bookstore opened in 1982, and, like Shakespeare and Company, it is one of the last independent, English-language stores in Europe. Open seven days a week. Monday 2pm to 7:30pm, Tuesday–Saturday 10am to 7:30pm, Sunday 1pm to 6pm. Village Voice Bookstore, 6 rue Princesse, Paris; Métro: Saint-Germain-des-Prés or Mabillon; Tel: 01 46 33 36 47; E-mail: query@villagevoice-bookshop.com; Web site: www.villagevoicebookshop.com.

Tea and Tattered Pages sells secondhand English-language books at decent prices. There is also a tearoom tucked inside the store. Open Monday–Saturday 11am to 7pm, Sunday 12pm to 6pm. Tea and Tattered Pages, 24 rue Mayet, Paris; Métro: Duroc/Falguière; Tel: 01 40 65 94 35; E-mail: mail@teaandtatteredpages.com; Web site: www.teaandtatteredpages.com.

Look for the secondhand and antique book market held in an old horse market pavilion in the Parc George Brassens on rue des Morillons in the 15th arrondissement of Paris (Métro: Convention). The Parc has vineyards, beehives, 510 rose bushes, walking paths, and more. The book market, held on Saturdays and Sundays from 9am to 6pm, has over over 200 participating booksellers, 68 of which rotate through each weekend.

In the warmer months used booksellers can be found lined up across the Seine River from Notre Dame Cathedral.

Literary Paris: A Guide, by Jessica Powell, covers thirty writers, as well as favorite cafés and literary landmarks. Part history, part guidebook, it is a worthwhile read for literature lovers.

Avignon

La Librairie Shakespeare maintains a tremendous selection of used books. Don't miss the tearoom, which serves tea and pastries with an English bent—expect scones, not croissants. Open Tuesday–Saturday 9:30am to 12pm, 2pm to 6pm. Shakespeare Books, 155 rue de la Carreterie, Avignon; Tel: 04 90 27 38 50; E-mail: shakespeareavignon@hotmail.com; Web site: shakespeare.bookshop.free.fr.

Visit Librairie Holstein, a French-language bookstore specializing in Buddhist philosophy. Librairie Holstein, 55 rue des Fourbisseurs, Avignon.

Montpellier

Book in Bar Café-Librairie is a bookstore and café featuring language conversation exchanges, English-language books, and a small inventory of used books. Book In Bar Café-Librairie, 8 rue du Bras de Fer, Montpellier; Tel: 04 67 66 22 90; E-mail: bookinbarmontpellier@orange.fr; Web site: www.bookinbar.com.

Ecobusinesses, Ecodestinations, and Places of Interest

From the lavender fields of Provence to the Turquoise Mediterranean coast and the wine regions, France offers many natural ecodestinations.

The French Ecotourism Association is a relatively new organization with about twenty business members that work on promoting responsible and ecological tourism. Currently, the resources on their Web site are somewhat limited, but the association itself offers good information. For more details, go to www.ecotourisme.info.

ORGANIC FARMS

There are more than 1,360,000 acres of land being officially farmed organically in France. There are plenty of farms to visit, and plenty of fresh organic food and products to eat. See Eating and Food and City and Regional Highlights for more organic farm locations.

For farm visits, explore regional *bio* organizations, maps, and information about producers at the Agriculture Bio Web site. Go to www.

La Fédération Nationale d'Agriculture Biologique des Régions de France (National Federation of Organic Agriculture for the Regions of France): www.fnab.org

Le Syndicat National (National Union of Organic Farming and Natural Food Processors): www.synabio.com

Demeter: Maison de l'Agriculture Bio-Dynamique (Demeter Biodynamic Farm Association): www.bio-dynamie.org

Centre National de Resources en Agriculture Biologique (National Center for Resources on Organic Agriculture): www.abiodoc.com

Biobourgogne Association (Organic Producers in Bourgogne) regional association: www.biobourgogne.fr

agriculturebio.org. Once there, click on the map for regional contacts, then access a local Web site and look for "Carte de Producteurs" to find farmers and stores selling certified organic products.

For over twenty years, rare vegetables have been grown at Le Potager d'un Curieux, a large ecological garden. Open Monday–Friday, March–October. There is no entrance fee. Plants and seeds are for sale at the garden, and at the Apt market. Jean-Luc Danneyrolles, la Moliere, Saignon; Tel: 04 90 74 44 68; E-mail: lepotager@wanadoo.fr.

For organic farms in the Alsace region, you can search on the Web site of the Alsace professional organic agriculture organization at www.opaba.org. Search under "Membres," "Les members operateurs," and "Les producteurs."

There are two farmer-driven organizations devoted to sustainable agriculture and changing the way people think about food and farming, with a focus on honoring the farmer, the land, the consumer, and the health of the earth. The Sustainable Agriculture Network (Réseau Agriculture Durable) was founded in 1994. For more information, go to www.agriculture-durable.org. The Confédération Paysanne is the French Farmers Association, which is a member of

Via Campesina, an international peasant movement promoting fair trade, sustainable agriculture, social justice, and environmental integrity. For more details about both organizations, go to www.confederationpaysanne.fr and www.viacampesina.org.

ORGANIC VINEYARDS AND WINES

It is hard to believe, but wine consumption is reported to be down in France, and some of the smaller vineyards are struggling. It seems that teens are drinking soda and beer instead of wine, and at the nightclubs they drink hard liquor instead of wine. Fathers have historically been in charge of instructing their children in the ways of wine, and as the divorce rate has climbed, this tradition has been impacted. In addition, France has cracked down on drinking and driving, curtailing wine drinking at lunch. All of these factors have greatly affected the wine industry, forcing France to take some drastic steps, including taking almost 200,000 acres of vineyards out of production, making France second to Italy in worldwide wine production. See the *Green Earth Guide* Map to Wine Regions in France on page 84.

In France, organic *(biologique)* vineyards *(vignobles)* represent approximately fifty thousand acres of two million total acres of vineyards. The Languedoc-Roussillon region was the first to develop organic vineyards, with the Bordeaux, Provence, and Burgundy regions following suit in recent years.

The harvesting of the grapes, called *les vendanges,* takes place for eight to ten days during September and sometimes into October, depending on the region and the weather. This is an extremely busy time for the vineyards. In mid-November there is a three-day celebration of the new vintage, and the Saint-Vincent Tournante, the festival feast day of the patron saint of winemakers, is held in late January.

Visits to organic vineyards are often welcome, but call ahead or check the appropriate Web sites for hours. The following information includes some of the best Web sites to visit when searching for organic wines and vineyards.

On the Eco-Bacchus Web site at www.eco-bacchus.com, you can search by region for the 659 vineyards certified as organic in France. Many of the organic vineyards do not have their own Web sites, so

Wine Regions of France

Eco-Bacchus serves as a database, providing the vineyard names, addresses, phone numbers, acres in production, the year the vineyards became organic, the wines they produce, and the organic certifying organization.

At the Fédération Nationale Interprofessionnelle des Vins de l'Agriculture Biologique (National Federation of Organic Wine Professionals), you can access lists of organic winemakers by region. For more information, go to www.fnivab.org.

The Bio-Bourgogne (Organic-Burgundy) organization has a great visual map showing all the organic producers in the Burgundy region. Organic wine producers are indicated by purple balloons on the map. Access the map directly at www.communitywalk.com/map/13634.

For organic wines and vineyards in Aquitaine, check out www. vigneronsbio-aquitaine.org. Search "carte geographique des vignobles" to find information about the sixty-nine organic vineyards in the region.

A few organic vineyards have their own Web sites, which can be very useful and informative for curious travelers.

Beaufort Vineyards Ambonnay Reims makes organic champagne. For more information, go to www.champagne-beaufort.sup.fr.

Vignoble Boudon is an organic Bordeaux vineyard. For details, go to www.vignoble-boudon.fr.

The Château Bousquette Web site can be found at www.chateaubousquette.com.

The Domaine du Vignes du Maynes, in the Burgundy region, has been organic since 1954. For more information, go to www.vignes-du-maynes.com.

BIODYNAMIC WINES

Biodynamic farming is based on the agricultural philosophies of Rudolf Steiner. While biodynamic farming includes organic farm management practices, it also uses specially prepared, natural treatments, incorporating natural rhythms and cycles of the moon and sun, light and warmth. Demeter Bio-Dynamie certifies biodynamic wines in France and lists biodynamic producers on their Web site. For more information visit Demeter: Maison de l'Agriculture Bio-Dynamique (Demeter Biodynamic Farm Association) at www.bio-dynamie.org.

Château la Canorgue is an organic and biodynamic vineyard located in Provence between Lourmarin and Avignon. The movie *A Good Year* was filmed at this vineyard. Open 9am to 7pm year-round, closed Sundays. Château la Canorgue, Rte du Pont Julien, Bonnieux, Vaucluse; Tel: 04 90 75 81 01; E-mail: chateaucanorgue.margan@wanadoo.fr.

Château Romanin is a biodynamic vineyard located outside of Saint-Rémy-de-Provence, northeast of Arles. They also grow almond and olive trees. The vineyard is certified by Demeter, Biodyvin, and Ecocert. Château Romanin; Tel: 04 90 92 45 87; Web site: www.romanin.com/.

Château Morillon is a biodynamic vineyard in the heart of Bordeaux. Château Morillon, Chantal and Jean-Marie Mado, Campugnan, Bordeaux; Tel: 06 76 41 14 18 or 05 57 64 72 75; E-mail: jmm@chateau-morillon.com; Web site: www.chateau-morillon.com.

Visit Wine Alchemy, a UK-based Web site about biodynamic wines from around the world, at www.winealchemy.com.

Gardening for Life—The Biodynamic Way: A Practical Introduction to a New Art of Gardening, Sowing, Planting Harvesting, by Maria Thun and Angelika Throll-Keller. Hawthorn Press, 2000.

A Biodynamic Farm, by Hugh Lovel. Acres, 2000.

Wine from Sky to Earth: Growing and Appreciating Biodynamic Wine, by Nicholas Joly. Acres, 1999.

Domain Weinbach is located in the Alsace region of France. Domain Weinbach, 25 Rte du Vin, Kaysersberg; Web site: www.domaine-weinbach.com.

For other biodynamic wine producers in France, see www.biodyvin.com. Click on "Les Adhérents," and then click on the list or map to find biodynamic wine producers. Similarly, visit www.vitis.org/biovins.html to find organic and biodynamic vineyards by French *département* numbers (see *Green Earth Guide* Map of France Departments, page 24).

SPECIALTY LIQUOR

Many local liqueurs are made in France. Pastis, one such specialty, is a French aperitif made from aniseed, vanilla, and cinnamon. The following local distilleries are in the Provence region, known for its variety of herbs on which the local liqueurs rely.

The Janot Distillery produces organic liqueurs, including Farigoulette Bio, made with thyme; Gentiane Bio, made with water, sugar, alcohol, maceration of gentian or thyme, and other herbs; and Pastis Janot Bio. You can find these liqueurs at some health food stores. Janot Distillery, Z.I. Les Paluds, Ave. du Pastre, Aubagne en Provence; Tel: 04 42 82 29 57; E-mail: infos@distillerie-janot.com; Web site: www.distillerie-janot.com.

In Pays de Forcalquier, located in Provence, the Distillerie et Domaines de Provence has been making aperitifs and liqueurs since 1898. They harvest herbs from Montagne de Lure, famous for its range of medicinal plants. April to December: Open Monday, Wednesday–Saturday 10am to 12:30pm, 2pm to 7 pm. July–August: Open Monday–Saturday 9am to 7pm, Sunday 9am to 1pm. Closed January–March. Distillerie et Domaines de Provence Tasting Room, 9 Avenue Sainte Promasse, 04300, Forcalquier; Tel: 04 92 75 15 41; E-mail: boutique@distilleries-provence.com; Web site: www. distilleries-provence.com.

The Domaine Alain Verdet is a twenty-acre vineyard, organic since 1971, which also makes small batches of organic Cassis (black currant liqueur). The Domain Alain Verdet, rue des Berdichrés, Arcenant; Tel: 03 80 61 08 10.

The painter Henri Manguin started a traditional distillery in Avignon in 1904, which specializes in pastis and eaux de vie ("waters of life"). Open Monday–Saturday 9am to 12pm, 2pm to 6pm. The Distillerie Manguin, 16 de la Barthelasse, Avignon; Tel: 04 90 82 62 29.

At the Abbaye Saint-Michel-de-Frigolet in La Montagnette, you can find Father Gaucher's "famous elixir" for digestion, which is made with thirty-three mountain herbs. Abbaye Saint-Michel-de-Frigolet in La Montagnette; Tel: 04 90 85 70 07.

BEER AND BREWERIES

In French, the words for beer and brewery are *bière* and *brasserie* (also a common name for café). For traditionally made, organic, and unpasteurized beer, try the Brasserie du Chardon. The brewery is located between Chambéry and Grenoble, east of Lyon. Open Tuesday, Thursday–Saturday 4pm to 8pm. Brasserie du Chardon, Impasse du Teura, ZA Les Fontaines, 38190, Bernin; Tel: 04 76 40 47 75; Web site: www.brasserie-du-chardon.com.

The Brasserie d'Uberach makes three organic beers. Open Monday–Friday 8:30am to 12pm, 1pm to 6:30pm. Brasserie d'Uberach, 30 Grand rue, Uberach, Alsace; Tel: 03 88 07 07 77; E-mail: brasserie. uberach@wanadoo.fr; Web site: www.brasserie-uberach.com.

The Brasserie de la Brière makes four micro-brewed, artisan beers, one of which is Thorella, a certified organic beer. Brasserie de la Brière le

Nézyl, Saint-Lyphard; Tel/Fax: 02 40 91 33 62; E-mail: brasserie.bri-
ere@wanadoo.fr; Web site: perso-orange.fr/brasserie-de-la-briere.

Brasserie du Canardou brews seven organic beers. Brasserie du Canardou, 24610, Villefranche de Lonchat; Tel: 05 53 80 55 54; E-
mail: canardou@wanadoo.fr; Web site: pagesperso-orange.fr/yves.
bou/brasseries/canardou.htm.

MINERAL SPRINGS

Some of the most famous names in mineral water come from France,
including Evian, Perrier, and Volvic. These and many other brands
are available throughout France.

Water "bars" are now popular in Paris. If you prefer to drink tap water and do not want to pay extra for bottled water, ask for *l'eau de
ville* (city or tap water). If you want carbonated water (water "with
gas" as it is sometimes called), ask for *eau gazeuse.*

Colette is an eclectic store in Paris with a range of products, free Wi-
Fi, and a water bar with over one hundred choices of water from
around the world. Colette, 213 rue Saint-Honoré, Paris; Métro:
Tuileries or Pyramides; Web site: www.colette.fr/.

Source Perrier is open seven days a week in July and August. From
September to April, Perrier is open by appointment Monday to
Thursday for a half-hour guided tour of the spring and production
facility. Source Perrier, Lieu dit les Bouillens, Vergèze; Tel: 04 66 87
61 01; E-mail: tourism-industriel-perrier@waters.nestle.com; Web
site: www.perrier.com.

WIND ENERGY

In French, wind, or wind energy, can be translated as *éolienne* or
vent, and *moulins à vent* means windmill. Wind power generation is
growing in France, and seeing a row of windmills from the window
of your train seat makes for a beautiful sight. See the *Green Earth
Guide* Map to Windsites on page 89 to see where windmills are situated in France.

There are twenty-four wind power installations all over France with
total current capacity at 1.3 gigawatts. To learn more, go to www.

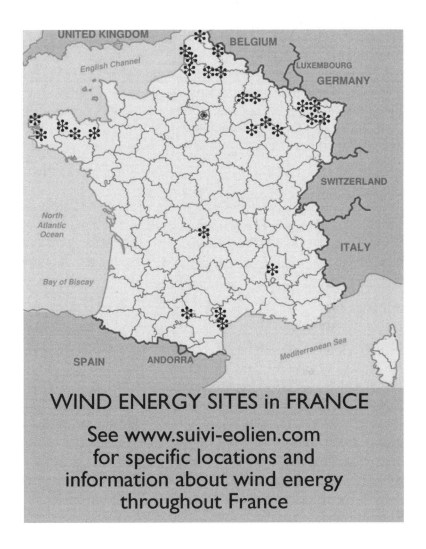

WIND ENERGY SITES in FRANCE

See www.suivi-eolien.com
for specific locations and
information about wind energy
throughout France

suivi-eolien.com. Other key Web sites for wind energy information in France include the French Wind Energy Association at fee.asso.fr, the Renewable Energy Organization at www.energies-renouvelables. org, and the Federation of Wind Energy at www.planete-eolienne.fr.

Many of the traditional, old-fashioned windmills were destroyed in World War II because they were easy, high targets. Since then, local mill organizations have been able to restore a number of mills. In the Nord–Pas-de-Calais, the northernmost part of France, a devoted group called the Association of Friends of Mills (ARAM) has restored forty-five mills. They also operate a museum and offer mill tours in French or English. ARAM, rue Albert Samain, Villeneuve d'Ascq; Tel: 03 20 05 49 34; Web site: asso.nordnet.fr/aramnord. For a complete list and description of the sites and mills, click on "les moulins rénovés" and "nos moulins." For photos of the mills, click on "Journée des Moulins" on the home page.

UNESCO World Heritage Sites

There are thirty sites in France on the United Nations Educational, Scientific, and Cultural Organization (UNESCO) list. Some are highlighted below and more are included under City and Regional Highlights.

Canal du Midi in Southern France is about 224 miles long. Completed in 1681, it was placed on the UNESCO World Heritage list in 1996. You can travel along the canal by boat, usually going no faster than five miles (or eight kilometers) per hour, which is a wonderful way to see old villages, vineyards, cafés, churches, and other sites. You will encounter sixty-four locks during the journey. The canal runs from north of Bordeaux through Toulouse to Etang de Thau, passing through Carcassonne (also a World Heritage site) and other villages on the tree-lined journey. Along the banks, you will see over 250,000 planted trees, many of them cypress. See www.canal-du-midi.org/en/ for maps, history, bike routes, and more detailed information about the canal.

Le trouve tout du Livre, an antiquarian bookstore on the shore of the canal, is a fun place to stop and visit. Le trouve tout du Livre, Mme Anne-Marie Gourgues, 28 allée de la Glacière, 11120 Le Somail France; Tel: 04 68 46 21 64; E-mail: trouve.tout.livre@wanadoo.fr; Web site: www.le-trouve-tout-du-livre.fr.

Listed as both a natural and cultural site, a rare dual recognition, the summit of Mont Perdu in the Pyrénées Mountains is 11,004 feet high (or 3355 meters). The Mont Perdu area includes two of Europe's largest and deepest canyons, which are located in Spain, and three cirque walls, which are located in France. See the *Green Earth Guide* Map to UNESCO Biosphere Reserves on page 124.

Pont du Gard is an ancient Roman aqueduct that originally spanned over one thousand feet. Some of the arches have disintegrated over the years, and although still quite impressive, Pont du Gard is shorter than it once was. Standing approximately 150 feet high, the bridge was part of an aqueduct that brought water from a spring in Uzes to Nîmes about thirty miles away. According to the tourist information, it took one thousand men and fifty thousand tons of stone to build the bridge, which was completed in AD 52. A newer section of the bridge has been built to match the old one, and you can walk across the bridge alongside the ancient aqueduct, which provides a great, close-up view of the original.

The expansive parking lot and walkways around Pont du Gard have been designed for a sea of summer tourists. If you don't mind the limited bus schedule and the closed gift shops, the off-season is a perfect time to visit the monument because you pretty much have it to yourself. If you decide to take the bus to Pont du Gard, be forewarned that this world-famous site rates an easy-to-miss bus stop on a highway rotary. The eastbound and westbound buses stop on different sides of the highway diagonally across the rotary. It is about a ten-minute walk from the bus stop to the entrance gate of Pont du Gard. Go to www.pontdugard.fr for more information and visiting hours.

The Vézère Valley contains over 147 prehistoric Paleolithic sites and twenty-five decorated caves, including the famous Lascaux cave paintings. The real Lascaux cave has been closed to the public because human breath was deteriorating the ancient cave paintings. Some six hundred feet from the original site, a replica cave with reproduction paintings has been built, and guided tours are available. Located on the Lascaux Hill just over a mile from Montignac, the cave is open almost all year except in January and early February. Like the cave near Les Eyzies-de-Tayac (about fifteen miles away), reservations are recommended, especially in the summer. More information is available at www.culture.gouv.fr/culture/arcnat/lascaux/en, the Web site for the French Ministry of Culture.

The walled city of Carcassonne was designated a World Heritage site in 1997 and has been well restored, making it an impressive fortress. The Canal du Midi runs by the city, and Carcassonne is on the train route between Toulouse and Montpellier. See more information under City and Regional Highlights.

The Abbey of Mont-Saint-Michel on the Normandy coast is one of the most photographed sites in France. See more information under City and Regional Highlights.

The city of Bordeaux, capital of the Aquitaine region in western France is designated as a United Nations World Heritage City. See more information under City and Regional Highlights.

Historical Sites and Other Sites of Interest

The National Archeological Museum is full of ancient artifacts. Musée d'Archéologie Nationale Château, place Charles de Gaulle, 78105, Saint-Germain-en-Laye; Tel: 01 39 10 13 00; Web site: www.musee-antiquitesnationales.fr.

Les Eyzies, "the prehistory capital," is in the Dordogne region of western France, and contains prehistoric cave sites, museums, parks, and other places of interest. For more information, go to the official tourist site at www.leseyzies.com, which also includes information about local *marché* (markets). The National Museum of Pre-History houses five million artifacts and keeps 18,000 of them on exhibit, including a 50,000-year-old child's skeleton, 30,000-year-old stone engravings, and 14,000-year-old bone carvings. The museum is open daily July–August, closed every Tuesday from September–June. The museum entry fee is around 6 euros; children under 18 are free. The National Museum of Pre-History, Dordogne, 1 rue du Musées, Les Eyzies-de-Tayac; Tel: 05 53 06 45 45; Web site: www.musee-prehistoire-eyzies.fr.

Within a few miles of Les Eyzies-de-Tayac are two prehistoric caves still open to the public: Font-de-Gaume and Combarelles, both of which date from between 12,000 and 14,000 years ago. Font-de-Gaume, less than one kilometer from Les Eyzies-de-Tayac on Route de Sarlat/D47, can be easily accessed on foot or by bike. Combarelles is just over two miles on D47, so it is also possible to walk or bike. In the summer months, reservations are recommended for these sites, as the number of visitors is limited to twelve at a time. The caves are closed on Saturday. Admission fee is approximately 8 euros; children under 18 are free. Call 05 53 06 86 00 or fax 05 53 35 2618.

The Niaux cave and the Prehistoric Art Park near Tarascon-sur-Ariège are open all year except during February, with variable hours and tour times. Unlike the Lascuax caves, the Niaux caves are still open to the public, but the number of visitors is restricted. Reservations are required. For more information, go to www.ariege.com/niaux.

Nîmes, once a major Roman city, is not far from the Pont du Gard, and you can catch a bus between the two sites. Nîmes, in the Languedoc-Roussillon region, has two very well preserved Roman buildings. The Arena, which holds 24,000 people, was built in the first century for gladiator events. It has been partially restored to host present-day bullfights. The Maison Carrée temple is one of most intact buildings from the Roman Empire and dates to AD 4. The deeply worn stone steps and weather-beaten walls of these sites come alive with history. If you are traveling between Nîmes and Avignon, I recommend the train rather than the bus—it takes half the time and costs half the fare of the bus.

The Camargue is one of France's regional nature parks. Located south of Arles, around Saintes-Maries-de-la-Mer, it comprises 250,000 acres of salt marshes and sand and salt dunes along the Mediterranean Sea. Natural sea salt from this area, harvested since Greek and Roman times, is sold in health and gourmet food stores around the world. Les Salins, the local salt company, prides itself on high quality pure sea salt harvested with the aid of the sun and wind. For more infotmation, go to www.salins.com. Their salt production facility, Les Salins du Midi, can be toured from March through October. Their salt brands include La Baleine (www.labaleine.fr), Le Saunier de Camargue (www.saunierdecamargue.fr), and Le Paludier (www.lepaludier.com), which is made without any chemicals or pesticides. For more information about the Camargue's extensive walking, biking and horseback riding trails, as well as the Parc Ornithologique du Pont de Grau, see **Wild and Natural Resources**.

Observatoire de Haute-Provence is an observatory in Provence with limited visiting hours. Observatoire de Haute-Provence; Tel: 04 92 70 64 00; Web site: www.obs-hp.fr/www/welcome.shtml.

The rich, natural ochre land in the Provencal towns of Roussillon, Gargas, and Rustrel is not to be missed. See more information under **Color and Art**.

Highlighted Sites and Cities

City and Regional Highlights

So much to see and so little time—this is the truth about France. The cities and regional highlights included here are merely a taste of all that France has to offer. To get a visual sense of where these sites are located within France, please see the *Green Earth Guide* Map of Highlighted Sites above.

Many maps and search options on Web sites refer to France's numbered *départements*. For navigation purposes, please remember that France has twenty-two regions, subdivided into ninety-five administrative *départements*. The *départements* are numbered and alphabetized. The city of Paris is arranged into twenty districts called arrondissements. These are like neighborhoods, but the arrondissement numbers do not necessarily correlate to named neighborhoods (such as the Latin Quarter). The last two digits of Paris zip codes contain the arrondissement number. All Paris zip codes begin with 750, and the last two numbers identify the arrondissement, so zip code 75004 is located in the 4th arrondissement, or the 4e, as it is sometimes abbreviated. See the *Green Earth Guide* Map of France Departments on page 24 and the *Green Earth Guide* Map of France Regions on page 23.

NICE

Don't miss the turquoise waters and stone beaches of Nice. Even in January, stalwart French people will take a constitutional swim in the turquoise water. Packed in the summer months, the Promenade d'Anglais runs the length of the beach. While walking, biking, or roller-blading along the promenade, you have a lovely view.

The Chagall Museum is a must-see. The airy and light museum, dedicated to Chagall's work, is filled with huge, breathtaking paintings depicting scenes from the Bible, as well as some of his earlier, smaller paintings. The museum is closed on Tuesday. From June to October the hours are 10am to 6pm, and from October to June the museum closes at 5pm. Take the #15 bus from the old part of the city. Musée National Message Biblique–Marc Chagall, avenue du Docteur Ménard, Nice; Tel: 04 93 53 87 20. ☞ green earth guide favorite.

Along the same route, but farther up the road, is the Matisse Museum. The Musée Matisse is a beautiful orange stucco building in a public park that is filled with olive trees and men playing serious *boules,* a French game played with friends that involves throwing metal balls on a dirt court. The museum has a great collection of Matisse's work from different periods in his life. The museum is a bus ride up the hill from the old center of the city. The museum is closed on Tuesday. The #15 bus goes to both the Matisse and Chagall museums. Musée Matisse, 164 avenue des Arénes de Cimiez, Nice; Tel: 04 93 81 0808.

Nice's historic old town is a warren of narrow, stone streets. In the heart of the old town and one block from the beach is Place Pierre Gautier, where different kinds of markets are held almost every day. On Sundays you will find the major weekly food and flower market. If you enter through the main gate on the beach side, the *bio* stands are located in the back right corner of the market. Nice has a youth hostel conveniently located in the old city about eight blocks from the market square (see more information under Accommodations). One of the French La Vie Claire health food stores, which has a large selection of gluten-free foods, including palmier pastries, is located around the corner from the hostel (see more information under **Food**).

PARIS

Paris is the largest city in France, and a list of important Parisian sites would fill a book. Included here are sites of note when traveling naturally, as well as a few of my favorites.

The Eiffel Tower and l'Arc de Triomphe, illuminated at night, make a spectacular vision. You can walk or take a short funicular ride to the Sacré-Cœur Basilica (see more information under **Sacred Sites**). The Grand Mosque is not to be missed (see details under **Restaurants**). There are outdoor movie screenings in La Villette Park (see more information under **Recreation**). The raised Promenade Jardin Plantée makes for great walking and views of Paris. Just below the promenade you will find the Viaduc des Arts and its fifty-one artisan stores and studios. Go to www.viaduc-des-arts.com for more information.

In Hebrew, the word "Shoah" means catastrophe and is used in French to refer to the Holocaust. Mémorial de la Shoah (The Shoah Memorial) is a museum dedicated to keeping the memory of the Holocaust alive. The names of the 76,000 French Jews who were sent to concentration camps are engraved on the Wall of Names to honor their memory. The memorial is free and open every day from 10am to 6pm, except Saturday, the Jewish Sabbath. Mémorial de la Shoah, 17 rue Geoffrey l'Asnier, 75004, Paris; Métro: Saint-Paul, Hôtel de Ville or Pont-Mare; Tel: 01 42 77 44 72; Web site: www.memorialdelashoah.org.

When visiting the city of love, light, and art, you should visit the Louvre and as many other museums as you possibly can. For travelers on extremely tight budgets, take heart. The official Paris Visitors

In London, the Tube announcers warn you to "mind the gap" between the train and platform. In France a "mind the merde" announcement should be broadcast over sidewalk speakers. While there is technically a pooper-scooper law in France, many French ignore it. There are dog droppings all over the sidewalks, and you really have to pay attention to avoid it.

Bureau Web site lists the twenty-two free museums throughout the city, as well as museums that have free days or free hours. For more details, follow the "Practical Paris" link at en.parisinfo.com/guide-paris/money/free-admission-and-good-deals/guide/free-admission-and-good-deals.

If you appreciate historic gravesites, you will enjoy the Cimetière du Père-Lachaise. Père-Lachaise is a large green space in the eastern part of Paris, which is wonderful for strolling and sightseeing. Home to the graves of many famous people, including Moliére, Chopin, Proust, Edith Piaf, Balzac, and rock star Jim Morrison, the cemetery also contains the graves of lesser-known luminaries who have greatly influenced the world of alternative medicine, including Samuel Hahnemann, father of homeopathic medicine and Claude Bernard, considered the father of physiology. You will also find memorials to the victims of three different World War II concentration camps. The cemetery is open daily from 8am to 6pm, Saturday from 8:30am to 6pm, and Sunday from 9am to 6pm. Cimetière du Père-Lachaise (Père Lachaise Cemetery), boulevard de Menilmontant, Paris; Métro: Père-Lachaise.

If you are fascinated by the underground infrastructure of a city, or by excrement, you can visit the sewer museum. The trip might also provide you with countless future jokes. If you do go, be prepared with a gas mask or scarf: It stinks—after all, it is a sewer. You will cross bridges over water rapids of sewage, and walk through puddles of condensation, which one hopes are not leaks. The signs warn you to not touch anything and to wash your hands after leaving. Open 11am to 4pm, closed Thursday and Friday. Paris Sewer Museum (Les Égouts de Paris), opposite 93 Quai d'Orsay, near the Alma-Marceau Métro.

Buy your tickets online for the Louvre and Orsay at www.louvre.fr/llv/ pratique/billetterie.jsp?bmLocale=en and www.musee-orsay.fr/en/visits/ admission/tickets.html. This will save you waiting in lines. If you do not buy tickets in advance, make sure you get to the Louvre first thing in the morning. Avoid the Orsay on Tuesday, when the Louvre is closed—the lines are daunting.

BRITTANY

Brittany, or *Bretagne* in French, is known for its locally produced sea salt, which makes the local butter and caramels especially delicious. You will enjoy Cap d'Erquy, a protected reserve with footpaths through the heather to beaches, pink sandstone quarries, and the *Lacs Bleu.* There are innumerable cliff and seaside walks with wonderful views. For more information, go to www.erquy-tourisme. com/index_gb.htm.

Walking along the Brittany coast on the GR 34, which runs about 360 miles and includes the Path of Lighthouses (Le Chemin des Phares), you can see twenty-three of the 111 lighthouses along this sixty-two-mile stretch of France's western-most coast. West of Rennes, you will find the Forêt de Paimpont (its ancient Celtic name is Brocéliande), which has fourteen lakes and is all that is left of a forest that used to cover the whole region of Brittany. Le Forêt de Paimpont is the literary home of Merlin's tomb and other Arthurian legends. La Fontaine de Barenton is considered Merlin's spring. See Sacred Sites for other Celtic and prehistoric sites in Brittany, as well as the famous ancient stone megaliths of Carnac.

Brittany is also home to the historic village of Quimper (pronounced "Camp-air"), four-and-a-half hours from Paris on the TGV train, where hand-painted, tin-glazed pottery called *faïence* has been made since 1690. You can tour the HB-Henriot faïence factory for 5 euros, Monday–Friday. Faïencerie HB-Henriot, rue Haute-Locmaria; 29337 Quimper; Tel: 02 98 90 09 36; Web site: www.hb-henriot. com.

Quimper has an indoor market in Les Halles Saint-François that is open every day. You will find open-air markets, too, including Le

Marché Biologique de Kerfeunteun at place Theophile Bonnemaison, boulevard des Frères Maillet, which is open on Fridays from 3:30pm to 7pm. For more information about organic foods in Brittany, go to the Brittany organic association Web site at www.interbiobretagne.asso.fr. Once there, click on "Les points de vente" to search for all the stores and markets selling organic products in the region.

At www.gites-de-france.com you can find 4200 rural *gîtes* (bed-and-breakfasts) and camping options for Brittany.

The walled city of Saint-Malo, not too far west from Mont-Saint-Michel (see more information under Normandy in City and Regional Highlights), provides majestic sea views from its one-and-a-half miles of ramparts. For details, go to www.ville-saint-malo.fr/decouvrir/en/index.html. Farther west you will find Cap Fréhel, a ragged point on the Emerald Coast (Côte d'Emeraude) with over 700 acres of wild land to explore. For more information, go to www.cap-frehel.net.

There are thirteen thalassotherapy centers and spas around the Brittany coast. For more information, see Clinics and Spas, the *Green Earth Guide* Map of Thalassotherapy Centers in France on page 71, and the *Green Earth Guide* Map of Baths and Spas in France on page 58.

The Seaweed Gatherer's Museum is known as the Musée de Goémoniers, part of the Ecomusée de Plouguerneau et du Pays Pagan. Admission is 4 euros. Check the Web site for visiting hours, which vary depending upon the season. Ecomusée de Plouguerneau et du Pays Pagan, Route de Kerveogan BP 35, Plouguerneau; Tel: 02 98 37 13 35; E-mail: bezhin@club-internet.fr; Web site: bezhin.club.fr/index.html.

NANTES

Nantes, France's sixth largest city, is a two-hour TGV train ride from Paris. Touted to be the greenest city in France, Nantes has over 110 miles of walking paths and over 180 miles of bike paths (see Bike Rentals for information about the inexpensive Nantes bike rental system). There are ninety-five parks in the city, and, at last count, 70 percent of all their waste is recycled. Nantes has the largest tram network in France, and they have a fleet of hybrid electric-powered tricycle taxis that provide low-cost, ecofriendly transportation called

Cyclopolitain. The main Web site, in French only, can be found at www.cyclopolitain.com, and reservations can be made by calling 04 78 30 43 42. For your convenience, the center of Nantes has wireless Internet.

Nantes has many markets open on any given day of the week, and the tourist office can provide you with information about all of them. The Talensac Market, open every morning, is a historical, covered market in Nantes that has been in operation since 1937. The organic market, Marché Bio du Bouffay, is held on Wednesdays at Place du Bouffay. Every Saturday morning from 7:30am to 1pm there is a flea market at place Viarme. On Tuesdays from 12pm to 7pm you can find used books on place de la Bourse.

Hammam Zeïn and Oriental Spa is a Middle-Eastern-style spa with steam baths. As with traditional hammams, there are separate hours for men and women. At Hammem Zeïn, women visit Monday, Wednesday, Thursday, and Saturday 1pm to 9pm, Tuesday–Friday 11am to 6pm. Men visit on Tuesday–Friday 6pm to 9pm. Families can come together on Sunday from 11am to 9pm. Open daily. Hammem Zeïn and Oriental Spa, Quai Ferdinand Favre; Tel: 02 40 89 00 99.

Nantes, the center of the Loire-Atlantique *département,* is just thirty-five miles from the Atlantic Ocean. Along the Loire-Atlantique coast there are four thalassotherapy centers. For full information visit the following Web sites: Daniel Jouvance at www.thalasso-danieljouvance.com; Alliance Pornic at www.thalassopornic.com/uk/cadre.htm; La Baule at www.thalasso-labaule.com; and Thalgo at www.lucienbarriere.com/localized/fr/thalasso_spa/nos_etablissements/thalgo.htm.

Detailed information about walking trails and routes are available through the tourist office. Bike routes along the Loire Atlantique Atlantic coast, called VeloOcean, can be found in a guide at the Nantes tourism office or online at www.nantes-tourisme.com/50699442/1/fichepagelibre/&RH=DEC_en&RF=DEC_AUTOUR-en. Click on the "Cycle Trails" link.

Nantes was an important city for the French Resistance network in World War II, and you will find a monument commemorating fifty executed Resistance prisoners. Nantes was also a major port in the French slave trade. In 1598, the Edict of Nantes, recognizing religious tolerance, was issued. Nantes is home to many museums, and the Old Palace houses an interactive museum. There are also many parks and gardens, including Jardin des Plantes, which is home to seventeen acres of rare plant collections, medicinal plants, and greenhouses. The Parc de la Beaujoire has four hundred varieties of magnolias. Iris and rose gardens cover over thirty-four acres. The GR 3 walking trail goes through Nantes and connects with the salt marshes of Guérande. Famous for its natural sea salt, still harvested by hand and sold as a specialty salt, Guérande is a walled city about fifty miles west of Nantes. For salt enthusiasts, you will enjoy the town's salt museum.

THE ISLAND OF NOIRMOUTIER

The Island of Noirmoutier in the Atlantic is considered to be part of the Vendée *département,* and lies to the south of the Brittany coast. The island specializes in fresh sea salt. It is known for its Passage du Gois—a 4.5-kilometer walkway connecting the island to the mainland, which is covered over by the tide twice a day. Walking and biking are the transportation of choice on the island. To find plentiful information about nature sites and walks, restaurants serving local food, and much more, go to www.ile-noirmoutier.com. There are salt marsh tours in the summer, including one that begins at a thatched shelter on the road to l'Épine, in front of Bois des Eloux, where you can buy local salt and salicornes pickles. You can also tour the marshes by canoe and visit L'Île aux Papillons, the Island of Butterflies.

LOURMARIN

Lourmarin is a historic village in Provence. You can take a bus to Lourmarin from Avignon, Apt, and Aix-en-Provence, but remember to pester the bus driver to make sure he stops at Lourmarin. And be sure to get off at the right stop. If you choose to drive a car in the summer months, be prepared to park outside the village and walk in, as there is very limited parking and Lourmarin is a popular destination. There are bed-and-breakfasts and *gîtes,* including the beautiful, luxury accommodations at Les Olivettes. Les Olivettes, Avenue Henri Bosco, Lourmarin; Tel: 04 90 68 03 52; E-mail: lourmarin@ olivettes.com; Web site: www.olivettes.com.

The village boasts five antique and secondhand stores, and multiple local artisans and artists. The Friday market, open until 1pm, has a wonderful, local *bio* stand. There is a sixty-two-acre organic herb farm, three kilometers from the village, called La Ferme de Gerbaud. From the village of Lourmarin, take Chemin (path) d'Aguye to Chemin de Gerbaud. The farm offers guided tours (in French or English) for 5 euros from April to October at 5pm on Tuesday, Thursday, and Saturday, and at 3pm from November to March. The farm store is open daily from 2pm to 7pm. La Ferme de Gerbaud, Campagne Gerbaud, Lourmarin; Tel: 04 90 68 11 83; E-mail: cgerbaud@aol.com; Web site: www.plantes-aromatiques-provence.com.

NORMANDY

In the Normandy region of northern France there are a number of sites of note. The world famous Abbey of Mont-Saint-Michel, a UNESCO World Heritage site, is over one thousand years old. Located on the western edge of Normandy, Mont-Saint-Michel, like Saint Michael's Mount in England, is a fortress-like abbey on an island with a rocky outcropping accessed by a causeway. Go to www.ot-montsaintmichel.com/horaires_gb.htm for information about parking and the tides, which are rumored to be the highest in continental Europe. You can buy entrance tickets online at mont-saint-michel.monuments-nationaux.fr/en.

Bayeux is an ancient town in Normandy filled with old stone houses and walls. Founded two thousand years ago, it has many buildings still standing from AD 1000–1500, including a large cathedral built in 1077. Home to the famous Bayeux tapestry, a wool-in-linen embroidered masterpiece spanning over two hundred feet, the tapestry tells the story of the conquest of England in 1066 by the Duke of Normandy, William the Conqueror. The tapestry museum is well worth the entry fee of 7 euros, which includes a great audio guide. For more information, go to www.tapisserie-bayeux.fr.

Bayeux somehow managed to escape damage from the Hundred Years' War, and even though it is only a few miles from the D-Day beaches lining the Normandy coast, it also survived the ravages of World War II. In Bayeux, there are museums, tours, and cemeteries commemorating World War II, and the D-Day sites of Omaha, Utah, Juno, and Gold beaches are between thirty and sixty minutes away. You will also find Le Mémorial des Reporters, a joint effort between Bayeux and the organization Reporters without Borders,* which honors freedom of the press and journalists from around the world who have lost their lives covering wars since 1944. There is a single headstone for the famous war photographer Robert Capa, who took extraordinary photographs of the D-Day landing while standing alongside the troops as they came off the boats.

Historically known for its lace-making, ceramics, and apple products, Bayeux boasts many local artisans carrying on the traditions of woodworking, lace-making, embroidery, porcelain and ceramic work, and stone sculpture. Local apple products are abundant here, including Calvados, an apple liquor, as well as cider, jelly, juice, and other goodies. Apple products made from local orchards surrounding Bayeux can be found at Cave Cidricole Lecornu, Place Charles de Gaulle, close to the cathedral. Open April–September 10am to 7:30pm, October–March 5pm to 7:30pm. For more information, go to www.lecornu.fr.

Bikes can be rented year-round at the Le Verger de L'Aure, impasse de L'Islet, conveniently located across from the Bayeux Tourist office, which is open 8am to 8:30pm. For more information, call 02 31 92 89 16. A booklet detailing nineteen walking or biking trails around Bayeux is available at the tourist office for 7 euros. Visit the Bayeux Office of Tourism at www.bayeux-tourism.com for area maps and more information.

The Jardin Public de Bayeux, in the northwestern corner of the town, has four hundred trees, including an old weeping beech listed as an historical monument. In the summer, you can spend over two hours walking through Le Labyrinthe de Bayeux in Mosles, located a few miles northwest of town. Go to www.labyrinthe-bayeux.com for more information.

Bayeux has seven secondhand and antique stores, which sell everything from traditional antiques to World War II artifacts that the locals still dig up on the nearby cliffs and beaches. Lovely, English-speaking Patricia Cowling runs a tiny store filled with treasures,

---

*Reporters without Borders, or Reporters sans frontières, is headquartered at 47 rue Vivienne, 75002 Paris; www.rsf.org. They publish an annual worldwide Press Freedom Index.

Brocante de Jolies Choses, on rue Larcher, across the street from the post office. Brocante de Jolies Choses, 7 Bis rue Larcher; Tel: 02 31 22 23 63.

While there are no health food stores in Bayeux, they can be found in the surrounding towns, which are accessible by car. Fresh produce, cheeses, and bakeries are abundant, and the Bayeux market, known for its excellent produce and products, is held on Saturday mornings in place Saint-Patrice. A smaller market is held on Wednesday mornings on rue Saint-Jean.

The local youth hostel is right across from the park Place Charles de Gaulle, in the heart of the old Bayeux village. The room I stayed in had a large French window that overlooked an old walkway and terrace, an old stone wall, and trees in the distance filled with singing birds. The wood and bamboo furnishings were comfortable, and the beds were made with the traditional rolled duvets. The hostel, quiet except for the lovely bird sounds, was pretty empty in February. However, the walls are thin, and I can imagine a less serene atmosphere when the rooms are full, the windows open, and late night summer partying is under way. Family Home is a member of the Hostelling International Network, but it has no e-mail or Web site, so you must book a reservation by fax or post. Beds are 19 euros per night. Family Home, 39 rue du General de Dais, Bayeux, Tel: 02 31 92 15 22; Fax: 02 31 92 5572.

There are bus tours to the various D-Day beaches, which cost approximately 45 euros, but you can take local buses for a fraction of the cost. For 2 euros, you can take the #70 bus from Bayeux village to the American cemetery and monument at Omaha Beach. It is only a thirty-minute bus ride, and in the winter, there is only one bus each way.

Omaha Beach is impressive and beautiful. It is a protected area, and the cemetery and monuments sit high above on a plateau. The acres of white crosses and Stars of David in the cemetery emphasize the magnitude of what happened on June 6th and 7th in 1944. Despite its sad history of war and wreckage, the beach is pristine now, littered only with seashells, golden sand, dramatic clouds, and an aura of significance.

Caen, a larger city about thirty minutes away from Bayeux (and two hours from Paris), was not as fortunate as Bayeux. As a major railway hub, it endured horrible bombing in World War II. Caen has museums, health food stores, and other attractions, but it does not have the old charm of Bayeux because most of the buildings are new. Friday morning is market day in Caen at place Saint-Sauveur, where the market has been held for almost one thousand years. Caen is home to the Museum of Peace or Le Memorial de Caen (www.memorial-caen.fr), and the D-Day beaches can be accessed from here as well as from Bayeux.

There are markets in almost every town in Normandy. You will find a market in Rouen on Tuesday, Friday, Saturday, and one on Sunday in place Saint-Marc. Shop in L'Aigle on Tuesday, and in Dieppe and Saint-Lo on Saturday morning. The marker in Forges-les-Eaux is open on Thursday and Sunday morning. For information about organic foods in Normandy, go to the Normandy organic association Web site at www.bio-normandie.org. Click on "Mangez Bio," "Guide des points de ventes," and "Manger bio en Basse-Normandie" to download the sixty-eight-page guidebook to organic food in Normandy. You can also click on "La Bio à la carte" to search by area for organic farms, markets, and stores.

AVIGNON

The walled city of Avignon, a UNESCO World Heritage site, is a good jumping-off point for touring Provence. Avignon is a small, fun university city, with many health food stores and restaurants (see more information under Food), and easy public transportation to towns in Provence and other regions in France. There are two train stations in Avignon. Avignon TGV, Avignon's stop on the high-speed TGV line, is a shuttle-bus ride away from the city. Avignon Centre is where most of the non-TGV trains depart and arrive, and it is across the street from one of the main gates of the walled city. The bus station is next door to the Avignon Centre rail station.

The Palais des Papes, Avignon's largest tourist attraction, is an impressive fortress that dates from the fourteenth century, when the Pope fled Italy and took up residence in Avignon. For more information see www.palais-des-papes.com/anglais/index.html. There is an old synagogue at Place Jerusalem where the pope offered protection to the Jews, who were being persecuted in France in the fourteenth century, accused of causing the Black Plague. Six hundred years later, with the protection of the Pope long gone, there was little sanctuary to be found. Inside, on one of the synagogue walls, is a list of Avignon Jews sent to Auschwitz. If you ring the bell at the side door, a kindly rabbi will greet you.

Biking and walking routes are plentiful in and around Avignon. You can walk up the hill past the Palais des Papes to a park that offers the best views of the Rhone River and the city of Avignon. For wine tours in the area, I recommend François Marcou. François is extremely informative, courteous, flexible, and good-natured —really the perfect combination for a tour guide. While his tours do not currently include organic vineyards, he is open to suggestions. And his wine tour motto is perfect: "You drink, I drive." For more information, visit www.avignon-wine-tour.com.

CARCASSONNE AND TOULOUSE

Carcassonne, a magnificent walled city about sixty miles southeast of Toulouse, is designated as a UNESCO World Heritage site. Markets are held on Tuesday, Thursday, and Saturday. If you are interested in walking through the fortressed city, you can find maps at www.carcassonne.org, the official city Web site. Trains to Carcassonne from Toulouse (about a one-hour trip) and Montpellier (about a two-hour trip) run ten to twenty-four times a day.

Toulouse, a university city centered between Bordeaux and Montpellier, has many markets, including a flea market on Sunday mornings. The organic food and flower market can be found Tuesday and Saturday mornings at the Place du Capitole. On Thursday there is an all-day book market at Place Arnaud-Bernard. Every day of the week you can find the fruit and vegetable market on boulevard de Strasbourg. Full of students, Toulouse has plenty of customers for its numerous secondhand stores *(le fripe),* including le Grenier d'Anais, a used vintage clothing store at 4 rue Peyroliéres. VéloToulouse is a new city-wide bike rental program, similar to Vélib' in Paris, with over 250 stations throughout the city. Tickets are available on a daily basis, or you can choose weekly, monthly, or yearly subscription options. Full details can be found at www.velo. toulouse.fr. The Canal du Midi runs through the city (see more information under **UNESCO World Heritage Sites**). The Arles Way, one of the routes to Santiago (see more under **Sacred Sites**), goes through Toulouse.

AQUITAINE

The Aquitaine region has some spectacular sites and natural resources. Bordeaux, the capital of Aquitaine, is a World Heritage site. It has more than twenty markets, including an organic market in front of the Saint-Pierre Church on Thursdays, and the Marché de Quais at Quai des Chartrons on the banks of the Garonne river, which runs through the city. Every Sunday morning there is a flea market at Saint-Michel. The area has more than four thousand châteaux and vineyards.

Covering 74,000 acres, La Forêt des Landes (Landes Forest National Park) is considered the largest maritime pine forest in Europe. You will find hiking and biking trails throughout the park, and canoeing opportunities on the park's lakes and rivers. For more information, go to www.parc-landes-de-gascogne.fr/. There are sixty-five miles of beaches along the Landes coast (Côte Landaise). For detailed information about every beach along the coast and safe places to swim, go to www.plages-landes.info. The Côte Landaise comprises the southern part of the Côte d'Argent, or the Silver Coast, which covers over 150 miles of sandy Atlantic Ocean beach—the longest stretch of straight shoreline in Europe. Don't miss the Dune de Pyla: rising over three hundred feet, it is the highest sand dune in Europe. The dune is approximately eight miles south of Arcachon, so you can bike or take a bus from the train station (bike rentals are available at the train station). In July and August these beaches are crowded but still magnificent. If you want a quieter scene, go in the off-season months—whole lengths of the coast are virtually empty.

ALSACE

The Alsace region is full of organic farms and natural sites. In Strasbourg, the Grande Île—the historic center of the city—is designated as a World Heritage site. Like most major cities, Strasbourg has many markets throughout the week. The organic market is in the forecourt of the Palais Rohan on Saturday mornings.

Alsace is known for its wines, and there are 103 organic vineyards, comprising 34 percent of the vineyards in Alsace. The following four Alsatian organic, biodynamic vineyards merit a visit: Eugene Meyer at 21 rue de Bergholtz Zell, Bergholtz, Tel: 03 89 76 1387; Pierre Frick biodynamic wines, Web site available at www.pierrefrick.com; Jean Baltenweck, a twenty-two-acre organic vineyard near Ribeauville; and Clément Klur at Vignoble (vineyard) Klur, 105 rue des Trois Epis, 68230 Katzenthal, Web site available at www.klur.net.

Organic markets can be found on Friday mornings in Turckheim, and in Colmar on Thursday and Saturday. Natural foods stores in the region include Sonnenbluem Coop in Colmar, Nature et Santé in Houssen, and Unis Vers Bio in Ingersheim. Unis Vers Bio on Route d'Equisheim is a Biocoop store, located only minutes away from the organic Klur vineyards in Katzenthal. Outside the village of Montagne, organic bread can be found at the Boulangerie Biologique Turlupain. Open Monday, Wednesday, and Friday 4pm to 7:30pm. Boulangerie Biologique Turlupain, 97 Tannach, Orbey; Tel: 03 89 71 28 30.

Run by the Conreau family, the farm store of Schoultzbach (also a working farm, *gîte,* and guesthouse) offers organic cheeses, wines, and other local products. The store is open Monday–Friday 2pm to 7pm, Saturday–Sunday 9am to 12pm, 2pm to 7pm. Schoultzbach, 284 Schoultzbach, Orbey; Tel: 03 89 71 33 68; E-mail: contact@ schoultzbach.fr; Web site: www.schoultzbach.fr. To find out more about organic Muenster and other cheeses from the biodynamic, Demeter-certified Les Pensées Sauvages, call 03 89 26 40 13. You can search for more organic farms on the Web site of the Alsace professional organic agriculture organization at www.opaba.org. Follow the links "Membres," "Les members operateurs," and "Les producteurs." You can locate health food stores using the same site by clicking on "Les producteurs" and "Distributeurs."

See the Natural Resources section for information about Alsace's special attractions, including Monkey Mountain, Eagle Park, and the Labyrinth. For hiking, see the Alsatian Club Vosgien under Hiking.

Burgundy, *Bourgogne* in French, is about two hours from Paris on the TGV train. The region is known for its wine, and there are a number of organic vineyards. Wine tastings, called *degustation,* are plentiful. See more about the Bourgogne Organic Wine association under Organic Vineyards and Wines. Biking and hiking routes run throughout Burgundy.

For organic food, you can visit the region's capital, Dijon, famous for mustard, where there is a daily covered market, Les Halles, designed by Gustave Eiffel, the man who designed the Eiffel Tower. One hour south of Dijon in Beune is a weekly market, with all sorts of local and organic food, which is held on Saturday, 8am to 1pm. In the old stone village of Brancion, the Marché Biologique is held the first and third Sunday of every month. In Cluny there is a weekly Saturday morning market with conventional and organic food.

Sacred Sites

France has an unusually high number of ancient stone structures, most of which date back to between 3500 and 2000 BC. Many of these stone structures are not listed in guidebooks; however, depending upon the town, some are listed as historical monuments.

The word "megalith" is a general term from the Greek meaning "great stone." Many single and grouped stones, and stone structures, dot the French countryside. Dolmens are megalithic stone structures that look like a giant table, with two standing stones and one stone resting horizontally across the top. Dolmens are thought to have been built as passageways or tombs. Menhirs are large upright stones, usually standing alone, whose purpose remains a mystery. Menhirs may have been used as territory markers or for religious ceremonies.

The Menhir de la Pierre Plantée, near Lussan north of Nîmes, measures 5.6 meters high, making it the tallest in southern France. Located near Nîmes in Gard, the Menhir de Courbessac is over two meters high and is approximately 2500 years old. In Hérault, there are more than 550 dolmens and 150 menhirs.

The megaliths of Locmariaquer are quite amazing and magical. The stone monuments include the Grand Menhir, originally over sixty feet tall, the Merchant's Table (Table-des-Marchands), a six-thousand-year-old stone chamber, and megalithic art engraved in stones at Pierres-plates and Mané-Rutual. Located in Locmariaquer, Brittany, the sites are open every day with an entry fee of 5 euros. For more information, go to locmariaquer.monuments-nationaux.fr/en/?fl_r=8 and www.culture.gouv.fr/fr/arcnat/megalithes/en/mega/megaloc_en.htm.

The Carnac megaliths can be found in Carnac, a seaside resort town near Quimper in northwest France. The ninety-eight acres of three thousand standing stones contains Celtic and neolithic ruins dating back over six thousand years. Web sites with the best information can be found at www.ot-carnac.fr and carnac.monuments-nation-aux.fr/en/. The Museum of Prehistory in Carnac houses over six thousand objects dating from prehistoric to Roman times. Open July through August 10am to 6pm; May, June, and September 10am to 12:30pm, 2pm to 6pm, closed Tuesday; October thorugh April 10am to 12:30pm, 2pm to 5pm, closed Tuesday. Musée de la Préhistoire, 10 Place de la Chapelle, 56340, Carnac; Tel: 02 97 52 22 04; Web site: www.museedecarnac.com.

Four routes go through France to Santiago de Compostela, Spain. These routes connect with two of the six routes in Spain that lead to the pilgrimage site of the tomb of Saint James the Apostle. You can walk on any section of the routes, but if you want to be considered an official pilgrim, there is a minimum distance you must travel—one hundred kilometers (62 miles) on foot or two hundred kilometers (124 miles) on bicycle. There are low-cost accommodations along all the routes for pilgrims only. For more information, go to the Web site for the Association de Coopération Interrégionale les Chemins at www.chemins-compostelle.com. You can find maps, route information, and you can download an official *credencial* for the route. The France routes include the Arles Way, or Via Tolosana, which runs almost 500 miles; the Le Puy-Sain-Jean route runs almost 450 miles; the Vezelay-Saint-Jean route runs about 480 miles; and the Paris-Saint-Jean route runs over 520 miles. See the *Green Earth Guide* Map to the Santiago Routes on page 111.

Other than the obvious sacred beauty of France's natural resources, France is home to many old churches and cathedrals, many of which

Routes to Santiago de Compostela, Spain ~
The Way of St. James

Vezelay 900 km
Tours 680km
Le Puy 750km
Arles 740km
Santiago de Compostela

are listed as UNESCO World Heritage sites. Below you will discover a few more unusual sites to visit and enjoy.

Mont Ventoux in the Vaucluse in Provence is considered a Celtic holy mountain and is recognized by UNESCO as a Biosphere Reserve. See Natural Resources for more information.

Other sites considered to have been holy Celtic areas include the Forêt de Coat-an-Hay and Forêt de Coat-an-Noz sacred forests, nestled in together west of Guingamp in Brittany, and the sacred forest of Forêt de Paimpont in Rennes (see Brittany under City and Regional Highlights). Located southeast of Rennes, La Roche aux Fées (The Rock of Fairies) is a megalithic structure measuring sixty-feet long and dating back to 3000 BC. Île de Sein, considered a pagan holy island, is accessible by boat from Audierne, almost due west of Quimper off of Brittany's coast. The sacred forest of Forêt de Huelgoat in the Montagnes d'Arrée (Arree Mountains) on the edge of the Parc Naturel Régional d'Amorique in Brittany is about thirty-six miles from Quimper.

Black Madonnas, also called Black Virgins, hold a fascination for people. France has a large number of Black Madonnas (or *Vierges Noires*), and each one is unique. Le Puy-en-Velay is the starting place for one of the routes to Santiago, and the Notre Dame du Puy Cathedral features a Black Madonna. Three kilometers north of Caen in Normandy there is a Celtic goddess site, and a Black Madonna rests in the basilica Notre Dame de la Délivrande. In Toulouse, one of the cities along the Arles route to Santiago (see more under Sacred Sites), the Daurade Basilica has a Black Madonna dating from 1807—the original one was burned in the French Revolution. At the Notre Dame des Neiges in Aurillac, Cantal, there is a Black Madonna from the sixteenth century. In Haute-Loire, the Notre Dame de la Chapelle Geneste also has a sixteenth-century Black Madonna. Rocamadour, an old village about one hundred miles north of Toulouse, sits perched in the rocky landscape. Rocamadour is a pilgrimage site with a cluster of chapels and churches, including the Chapelle de Notre Dame, which houses a Black Madonna dating from the ninth century. It is open daily from 9am to 7pm. The Web site, in French, can be found at www.notre-dame-de-rocamadour.com.

In Paris, the Sacré-Cœur Basilica comes alive when the nuns sing vespers at six o'clock every evening. On Sunday, vespers begin at four o'clock. Please be respectful when visiting—it is amazing how many people talk and take pictures even when the signs say both are prohibited. For more information, go to the Sacré-Cœur Web site at www.sacre-coeur-montmartre.com. ☛ green earth guide favorite.

Color and Art

Through the ages, France has been known for its great artists and artwork, so it is not surprising to find special sites dedicated to natural colors, artists, and art supplies.

In Paris, the historic Sennelier art store, in existence since 1887, can be found by walking across the bridge over the Seine to Quai Voltaire. The small, but packed store is famous for catering to Cézanne and Picasso, and the Sennelier brand is particularly known for its large assortment of pastels. Open Tuesday–Saturday 10am to 12:45pm, 2pm to 6:30pm; Mondays 2pm to 6:30pm. ☛ green earth guide favorite.

There are other Sennelier stores at 4 rue de la Grande Chaumière and at 6 rue Hallé, but these are new, not historical. Sennelier, 3 Quai Voltaire/Couleurs du Quai Volatire; Métro: Palais Royal Le Louvre; Web site: www.sennelier.fr.

In Nice, as well as in Marseille and Cannes, there is a wonderful art store called Bruno Charvin Arts Toiles et Couleurs. The Charvin Arts stores have a huge selection of materials and tools for artists—easels, pastels, paints, papers, brushes, and more—with particularly beautiful house-brand paints that capture the colors of the Provencal Mediterranean area, including yellow ochre, violet-blue, and all manner of blues and greens. Bruno Charvin Arts Toiles et Couleurs, 39 rue Gioffredo, Nice; Tel: 04 93 92 92 82. ☞ green earth guide favorite.

Roussillon is a photographer's heaven, especially in the late afternoon. The deep blue of the sky juxtaposed with the red and orange buildings that fill the village is magnificent. The village of Roussillon sits on Mont Rouge and was the center of ochre production until World War II. At the bottom of the village there are walking paths—called Le Sentier des Ocres—through the ochre cliffs. The paths remain open only during the weekends in the winter, but they stay open from 9am to 7pm all week during high season. The roughly forty-minute walk is well worth the admission cost of 2.50 euros. Be warned: Do not wear white or light-colored clothes unless you want to look like an ochre pastel when your walk is finished. Roussillon is unique in the world and not to be missed. The official tourist office for Roussillon can be found at www.roussillon-provence.com.

The Conservatory of Ochre is about three kilometers down the road from the village of Roussillon. The first building in the Conservatory complex houses an extensive bookstore where classes are held year-round in painting and special ochre applications. Below and behind the bookstore is L'ancienne usine Mathieu, a series of museum displays of an old ochre processing factory. Another building in the complex houses the pigment and art supply store—a painter and artist's dreamland. Walls lined with jars of natural and synthetic pigments make a colorful and inspiring display. The conservatory ships the natural, powdered pigments to artists and artist supply stores around the world. The natural ochre colors range from muted yellows to reds and browns. Open seven days a week. The Conservatory of Ochre, Route d'Apt D-104, Roussillon; Tel: 04 90 05 66 69;

E-mail: info@okhra.com; Web site: www.okhra.com. ☞ green earth guide favorite.

You can buy ochre in powder and pastel form in Apt at Ets Chauvin, a small, funky warehouse-style store with sacks of natural and synthetic powdered colors lining the walls and displays, located a few blocks walk from place Saint-Pierre in Apt. Open Monday–Saturday year-round. Ets Chauvin, Route de Viton, 84400 Apt; Tel: 04 90 74 21 68; Web site: www.ocreschauvin.fr.

You can also purchase ochre at Les Ocres de France, which is open only on Saturday mornings in July and August. The rest of the year they are open from Monday to Friday with the customary closing for lunch from 12pm to 2pm. Les Ocres de France, Ets Guigou 526 avenue Victor Hugo, Apt; Tel: 04 90 74 63 82; E-mail: ocres-de-france@wanadoo.fr; Web site: www.ocres-de-france.com.

Ochre is no longer mined at Roussillon. The sole remaining ochre mine is in Gargas, a neighboring village. You can visit the factory and the mine in Gargas on Fridays with advanced booking. Admission is 6 euros. Call 04 90 74 12 70 for more information. The exposition *Terre d'Ocres, Fragments de Mémoire* ("The Ochre Industry: Past and Present") is open Monday, Tuesday, and Thursday 9am to 12pm, 4pm to 6pm. Admission is 3 euros.

Ochre mine remnants can be found at Le Colorado de Rustrel (or Le Colorado Provençal) in the Parc Naturel du Luberon, the red, orange, and gold cliffs from the old ochre mines in the Luberon area. There are seven Sentiers de Ocriers (ochre pathways) varying in length from about half a mile to eight miles. The walking trails are free, but you must pay for parking in the lots off of highway D22. Maps are available at the tourist office, and you can purchase a book about the ochre trails for 4.60 euros at the tourist office and Rustrel Town Hall. Remember: The ochre will get on your clothing and shoes, so avoid wearing anything you do not want dusted with ochre. For more information, go to mairie.rustrel.net.

If you want longer hikes through the ochre area, there are three long-distance trails that wind through the area: GR6, GR97, and GR9, which are marked in red and white. There are biking trails marked by other colored signs: Green signs run through the towns of Apt, Gargas, Roussillon, Villars, Rustrel; red ochre signs go through the same

Ochre is stunning, and it has been used for millennia. Some of the earliest known cave art was drawn with charcoal and ochre, and the Australian Aborigines have used it in their art for centuries. Much new Aboriginal art is painted with synthetic ochre colors. It is said that because they consider natural ochre to be sacred, the artists use natural ochre only for the paintings they keep. See plates 11–14.

towns, but in a different configuration through Apt, Rustrel, Villars, Roussillon, Gargas; and the yellow ochre signs link the green and red paths. Maps of the bike routes are available at local tourist offices. The Web site www.ocresenvelo.com is under construction, but when complete it will offer online maps.

Terres et Couleurs, based in Paris since 1995, is a nonprofit organization promoting the use of natural color pigments, such as ochre, sienna, and green earth. The Web site does not sell pigments, but they do provide information about colored earths, great photos of mines, and lists of dealers around the world. Go to www.terresetcouleurs.com for details.

Solargil is a Web company in France specializing in products for ceramics and pottery. They sell ochre, hematite, and other earth pigments. For more information, go to www.solargil.com.

In the Ardennes region of northern France, there is one site where sienna pigment is still excavated. You can purchase the sienna and other natural pigments at Le Moulin a Couleurs (The Color Mill), Hameau Bonne Fonatine, Ecordal, Ardennes, Tel: 03 24 71 22 75; E-mail: moulincouleurs@wanadoo.fr; Web site: pagesperso-orange.fr/moulincouleurs/pageG.htm.

In Aix, Provence, you can see Cézanne's studio, and his palettes and tools, but no paintings. The studio is located two miles from the city center. From the Rotunde stop in front of the Saint-Christophe Hôtel, you can take the #1 bus to the Cézanne stop, which leaves every twenty minutes. The tourist office in Aix provides a map and itinerary that lets you "follow in Cézanne's footsteps" throughout Aix, or you can find a map on the Atelier Cézanne Web site at www.atelier-cezanne.com. Atelier Cézanne, 9 Avenue Paul Cézanne, Aix; Tel: 04 42 21 06 53.

There are a number of health food stores in Aix, including La Vie Claire, which is open Monday–Saturday 7:30am to 1pm, 2:30pm to 7:30pm. La Vie Claire, 49 rue d'Italie, off boulevard du Roi Rene; Tel: 04 42 38 23 73. You can visit the Biocoop and Bonneterre Web sites (see the Food section) for other health food stores in Aix, and be sure to use Bouches-du-Rhône #13 as the *département* for your search.

Arles is a fun and funky small city, famous for its great markets, Roman ruins, and for being home to van Gogh for a brief period in his life. A downloadable map of the city is available at www.tourisme.ville-arles.fr/document/pdfs_document/plan_centre_ville_arles.pdf. Information about the van Gogh walking tour is available at www.tourisme.ville-arles.fr/us/a4/a4a.htm. Please note that the van Gogh Foundation does not display van Gogh's work, but rather displays the work of artists inspired by van Gogh. However, the gift shop of the foundation does sell van Gogh prints and postcards. For more information, go to www.fondationvangogh-arles.org. One of the La Vie Claire health food stores can be found around the corner from the Yellow Café, at 3 rue du Docteur Fanton. It is open 8:30am to 12:15pm, 2:30pm to 7pm. Or you can buy food at the Wednesday and Saturday markets, which are open until noon.

For Monet lovers, visit the Fondation Claude Monet at rue Claude Monet, Giverny, to see the artist's house and gardens. The gardens are open from April 1 until the end of October. The Web site offers a calendar detailing which flowers bloom when, as well as a wealth of information about transportation, nearby accommodations, and the locations of Monet's paintings. Go to giverny-monet.com for more information. You can reach the Vernon train station from Paris (take the Rouen line) in less than an hour. From the Vernon train station you can take a shuttle bus for 4 euros, rent a bicycle, or walk to Giverny, which is 4 kilometers away. See the Web site for directions, as there is a special route for bikes and walkers that is different from the car route.

Aroma in France

There are many aromatherapy museums, farms, and schools in France, particularly in Provence.

Musée des Arômes et du Parfum de Graveson-en-Provence is a museum, organic farm, and school that features native aromatic plants and produces amazing products. Open 365 days a year, 10am to 12pm, 2pm to 6pm. Admission is 4.50 euros. A car is recommended for reaching the museum and farm, which is located slightly off the beaten path. Also see the associated Aroma Cocoon Spa under Clinics and Spas. Musée des Arômes et du Parfum de Graveson-en-Provence, ancien chemin d'Arles, Graveson-en-Provence; Tel: 04 90 95 81 72; E-mail: info@museedesaromes.com; Web site: www.museedesaromes.com.

Learn more about aromatherapist and author Nelly Grosjean at www.nellygrosjean.com. Nelly Grosjean's books contain a wealth of information. One of her books, *Aromatherapy from Provence,* has been translated into English. Her bio body care line can be found at www.biossentiel.com and her bio essential oils are Vie Arome (see Essential Oils) www.viearome.com. ☛ green earth guide favorite.

Essential Oil Resource Consultants offer courses, adventures, resources and information, and a research database about aromatherapy and essential oils. Essential Oil Resource Consultants, Au Village, 83840 La Martre, Provence; Tel: 04 94 84 29 93; E-mail: essentialorc@club-internet.fr; Web site: www.essentialorc.com.

Doctor Valnet's essential oil single and combination preparations, made from organic plants, are sold in pharmacies throughout France. Search the Web site for stores that carry these oils in any region. Laboratoire d'aromathérapie Cosbionat, 1 rue du Mons BP 94, 41106 Vendôme; Web site: www.aromatherapie-valnet.com.

Florial France Florihana distillerie is a distillery, school, shop, and organic farm selling organic essential oils, hydrosols, oils, tinctures, and herbs. Florial France Florihana distillerie, Les Grands Prés, 06460 Caussols; Tel: 04 93 09 06 09; Fax: 04 93 09 86 85; E-mail: info@florial.com; Web site: www.florihana.com; English Web site: www.florihana.com/en/.

Grasse is considered the perfume capital of the world. While perfumeries abound, Grasse originally was known for its soil—perfect for jasmine, hyacinth, and other delectable scented flowers. Annual festivities include the Aromatherapy fair in May; the Venusia Beauty and Well Being Fair in April; and the International Rose expo in May. August is the Jasmine Festival, and September is the Bio Grasse (Organic Products) Festival and Fair (see the *Green Earth Guide* French Festivals and Events Calendar on pages 26–27). Getting to Grasse from Nice by bus is a bargain, and it is a safe bet as far as French buses are concerned: you leave from the bus station in Nice and arrive at a smaller bus station in Grasse. The bus trip takes one-and-a-half hours and costs between one and two euros each way. There are regular buses throughout the day.

Fragonard and Molinard are the most visible perfumeries with free tours, and both have magnificent artifacts from the history of perfume. Fragonard is the most accessible. Molinard is down (and back up) a hill. The city of Grasse is a little dingy, but it sits high in the hills and the views are spectacular. You can get an English map *(carte anglais)* at the tourist office on the main street of boulevard de Jeu de Ballon, down the hill from the bus station. The Fragonard Museum is just down the steps from the tourist office. If you are looking for health food while touring Grasse, there are two options: La Vie Claire, which is southwest of the Molinard Museum; and Natur Marché, which is southeast off of the Route Cannes. The only drawback is that both stores are outside the main town and require a car to reach. Natur Marché Grasse, 57 boulevard Marcel Pagnol; Tel: 04 92 42 48 47. La Vie Claire, 67 avenue de la Libération; Tel: 04 92 42 02 62.

The Museum of Grasse is open year-round, but keeps limited hours in the winter. The museum has collections and exhibits covering the history of perfume, scent, and cosmetics. The Museum of Grasse, 8 place du Cours, 06130, Grasse; Tel: 04 97 05 58 00; Web site: www.museesdegrasse.com.

While scent and perfume companies fill the city of Grasse, I have included here a few that specialize in natural fragrances.

Laboratoire Monique Rémy, part of International Flavors & Fragrances, specializes in the production of natural raw materials for the perfume and flavor industry, including mosses, jonquils, narcisse, blackcurrant buds, clary sage, lavender, lavandin, and hay—yes, they make a pure extract of hay! The natural scents are extracted and concentrated into essential oils, concretes, absolutes, resinoids, and into molecular, distilled, and terpenless products. Laboratoire Monique Rémy, Parc Industriel des Bois de Grasse, 06130, Grasse; Tel: 04 92 42 43 44; Web site: lmr@labo-remy.com.

Ecocert-certified, Charabot was founded in 1920. It began selling bitter orange peels *(coulanes),* and grew into distilling and extracting local plants and flowers, such as rose, jasmine, néroli, mimosa, violet, and iris. The stills are located at Pégomas, and the company headquarters are in Vallauris. Charabot, 10 avenue Yves Emmanuel Baudoin BP, Grasse; E-mail: contact.charabot@charabot.fr; Web site: www.charabot.fr.

Fragonard's Perfume Museum has an extensive array of perfume artifacts dating back to ancient Egypt, the Orient, and Europe. It is a worthwhile visit for any one interested in the history of scent and the origins of the perfume industry, which, up until World War II, used natural plants as the sources for perfumes. Open 9am to 6pm daily, except November–January, when it closes from 12:30pm to 2pm. Admission is free. Parfumerie Fragonard, 20 boulevard Fragonard, Grasse; Tel: 04 92 42 34 34; Web site: www.fragonard.com.

ESSENTIAL OILS

Organic essential oils are plentiful in France, and some of the many brands are listed here. These can be found in health food stores, specialty and cosmetic shops.

La Drôme Provençale makes organic essential oils, herbal remedies, Bach flower remedies, and other personal care products. La Drôme Provençale, ZA de Cocause, 26150 Die; Tel: 04 75 22 30 60; E-mail: infos@drome-provencale.com; Web site: www.drome-provencale.com.

Florame manufactures aromatic diffusers and organic essential oils. They have three stores in France, located in Montpellier, Saint-Rémy-de-Provence, and Paris. The Saint-Rémy store also has a museum. For more information, go to www.florame.com.

Les Simples is a local cooperative company making essential oils from organic or wild-harvested plants. Les Simples, Ciamp-Long, 06470 Guillaumes; Tel: 04 93 55 57 71 or 06 98 14 69 09.

At the Apt market in Provence you can fnd the local Herbes Sauvages de Haute Provence (Wild Herbs of Provence) essential oils and hydrosols, which have been ecologically grown and harvested since 1975. Herbes Sauvages de Haute Provence, Claude Mabille, 04200, Les Omergues; Tel: 04 92 62 0172.

Vie Arome sells organic essential oils, hydrosols, base oils, perfumes, books, and more. Vie Arome is affiliated with both the Aroma Cocoon spa, listed under Clinics and Spas, and the Musée des Aromes Graveson-en-Provence listed above. Vie Arome, 07340 Peaugres; Tel: 04 75 34 76 54; E-mail: info@viearome.com; Web site: www.viearome.com. ☛ green earth guide favorite.

Other French essential oil brands include Le Gattilier, Biofloral, Sanoflore, Martinetti, as well as small, local producers.

ESPECIALLY LAVENDER

For the true lavender aficionado and lover, you have hit pay dirt in Provence—this is the heart of the finest lavender production in the world. Museums, farms, products—all things lavender are abundant. The Apt/Sault area produces 20 percent of France's lavender. True lavender grows at high altitudes, and the hybrid lavandin grows at lower altitudes. Lavandin has a higher percentage of camphor, tends to have a more pungent aroma, and produces far more essential oil per plant. For these reasons, it is used more commercially and tends to be far cheaper than real lavender. Lavandin also tends to be more stimulating, whereas true lavender is calming.

The Lavender Garden has a collection of 160 varieties of *Lavandula,* which you can see from the end of June until early September when the plants are flowering. Open April 15–October 15. The Lavender Garden (Le Jardin Conservatoire de la Lavande), Route du Mont Ventoux, 84390 Sault; Tel: 04 90 64 13 08; E-mail: info@la-ferme-aux-lavandes.com; Web site: www.la-ferme-aux-lavandes.com.

The Lavender Museum covers the history, production, and products of lavender. There are displays of distillation equipment from the sixteenth century to the present day, and movies about lavender production. You will find a gift shop, picnic area, and, in season, a blooming lavender field. Closed in January. Open 9am to 12:30pm, 2pm to 6pm, with slightly extended hours from April to September.

Lavender Museum (Le Musée de la Lavande), Rt de Gordes D2, 84220 Coustellet; Tel: 04 90 76 91 23; E-mail: contact@museedela-lavande.com; Web site: www.museedelalavande.com.

The Lavender Festival (Lavande en Féte-Sault) is the largest of the lavender festivals. Held in mid-August, all things lavender are cele-brated, enjoyed, and sold. Sault, a World Heritage city, is surrounded by fields of lavender and wheat, and is not to be missed by the true lavender lover. E-mail: info@saultenprovence.com; Web site: www.saultenprovence.com.

The Abbey de Sénanque, surrounded by lavender fields, is one of the most picturesque lavender scenes and is frequently photographed. Worth a visit in lavender season, the abbey is near the historic village of Gordes. If you want to go inside the abbey, visit the Web site first, as it is a working abbey and hours are limited. For more information, go to www.senanque.fr.

Lavender Highlights

Don't miss the lavender honey *(miel)* made at La Miellerie du Mas des Abeilles in Bonnieux.

Visit a biodynamic farm offering lavender spa therapies at Ferme de Baume Rouse, 26400 Cobonne; Tel: 04 75 25 08 68; Web site: www.lafermedebaumerousse.net.

Other spas and thermal baths offer a variety of treatments, includ-ing massages, saunas, and whirlpools with lavender essential oil. See **Thermal Baths and Spas** for more information.

Probably the single most useful source of information about lavender in Provence—including walking routes, farms, distilleries, and prod-ucts—is the *Routes de Lavande* brochure, which can be downloaded at www.routes-lavande.com. It offers five travel circuits through dif-ferent villages, highlighting lavender fields, farms, distilleries, and products, as well as spas and services.

Please keep in mind that most of the farms and distilleries are open only during the summer months.

Château du bois Les Espagnols offers a walking tour through almost two hundred acres of lavender fields, and a distillery tour. Château du bois Les Espagnols, Lagarde d'Apt; Tel: 04 90 76 91 23.

Lavender blooms from June to August, depending on variety and location, and is harvested and distilled into essential oil from mid-July until the end of August.

Lavender is part of the *Lamiaceae* or *Labiatae* family, commonly known as the mint family. There are well over thirty species of the genus *Lavandula,* but the most common are listed below.

True Lavender is the common name for *Lavandula angustifolia* (also referred to as *Lavandula officinalis* and *Lavandula vera*). True Lavender is also known as English Lavender or French Lavender. The properties of True Lavender are relaxing, sedating, and hypotensive.

Spike Lavender is the common name for *Lavendula latifolia* (also referred to as *Lavandula spica*). Spike Lavender properties are stimulating and expectorating.

Stoechas Lavender is the commom name for *Lavandula stoecha,* sometimes called Spanish Lavender, and it has properties similar to Spike Lavender.

Lavandin is the common name for *Lavadula intermedia* or *hybridia* (also *Lavandula fragrans* and *Lavandula delphinensis*). Lavandin is a hybrid variety of Spike Lavender and True Lavender.

Lavande 1100 offers tours of the distillery, demonstrations, organically grown lavender, and beekeeping. Lavande 1100 D34 Lagarde d'Apt; Tel: 04 90 75 0142.

Jean-Claude Guigou Distillery offers free guided tours from July 15–August 25. Jean-Claude Guigou Distillery, Hameau les Agnels, Route de Buoux, 84400 Apt; Tel: 04 90 74 34 60.

Les Coulets Distiller offers a free tour of a traditional lavender distillery on a farm. Visits available from July 15–August 31 9am to 12pm, 1:30pm to 7pm. Les Coulets Distiller, Route de Rustrel D-22l, Apt; Tel: 04 90 74 07 55.

Distillerie du Vallon also offers free tours. Distillerie du Vallon, Le Vallon, Route des Michouilles, 84390 Sault; Tel: 04 90 64 14 83.

GAEC Aroma'Plantes is an organic farm offering distillery tours, as well as information about aromatherapy, lavender essential oil, and other aromatic and medicinal plants on the slopes of Mont Ventoux. GAEC Aroma'Plantes, Route du Ventoux, 84390 Sault; Tel: 04 90 64 04 02.

Musee de la Lavande-Distillerie is in Les Gorges d'Ardèche, north of Vaucluse. Open 10am to 7pm every day from April–September. Please note: Musee de la Lavande-Distillerie should not be confused with the Musee de la Lavande in Coustellet. Musee de la Lavande-Distillerie, D490, St-Remeze; Tel: 04 75 04 37 26; Web site: www.ardechelavandes.com.

Les Agnels is open July 15–August 25. Les Agnels, Hameau Les Agnels, Rte de Buoux, Apt; Tel: 04 90 74 34 60.

Wild and Natural Resources

France is full of breathtaking natural resources. Thankfully, the French government has protected many such areas, making them into regional and national parks. For information about the nine national parks and the forty-six regional parks in France, go to www.parcsnationaux-fr.com and www.parcs-naturels-regionaux.tm.fr. To learn more about France's natural reserves, go to www.reserves-naturelles.org/accueil/accueil.asp. See the *Green Earth Guide* map to Regional Parks on page 127.

France has ninety-seven botanical gardens *(jardins botaniques)*. For more information, go to www.bgci.org/jbf/. In Paris, the Promenade Jardin Plantée is a tree-lined promenade along a raised boulevard, which provides great views of Paris (Métro: Bastille/Ledru-Rollin, and not far from Gare de Lyon). With eighty-six acres, the Parc de la Villette is the largest green space in Paris (Métro: Porte de Pantin).

Paris has approximately four hundred gardens and parks of varying sizes. The Jardin Sauvage Saint-Vincent is a special garden with very limited hours. No pesticides are used in this park and wild flowers are plentiful. Open April–October, Saturdays 10am to 2:30pm, 1:30pm to 6:30pm. Jardin Sauvage Saint Vincent, rue Saint-Vincent; Métro: Lamarck-Caulaincourt.

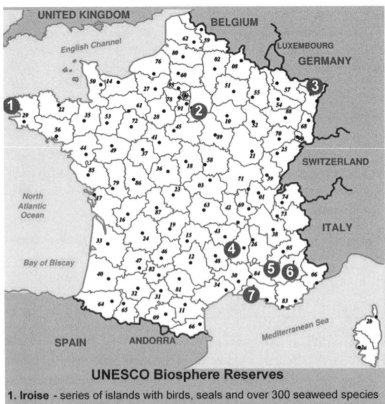

UNESCO Biosphere Reserves

1. **Iroise** - series of islands with birds, seals and over 300 seaweed species
2. **Pays de Fontainebleau** - Deciduous forest with over 5800 plant species
3. **Vosges du Nord** - Forest, wetlands and bogs with lynx and falcons
4. **Cevennes** - Forest and agriculture
5. **Mont Ventoux** - Flora, fauna and sacred site
6. **Luberon** - Two parallel mountain ranges with flora and fauna
7. **Camargue** - wetlands, sand dunes and bird sanctuary

See www.unesco.org/mab/BRs.shmtl for more information
about Biosphere Reserves and the France sites

The Regional Nature Park of the Volcanoes of Auvergne features great hiking trails and four volcanic massifs ranging from 4792 to 6188 feet high. The Regional Nature Park of the Volcanoes of Auvergne, Montlosier, 63970 Aydat; Tel: 04 73 65 64 00; Web site: www.parc-volcans-auvergne.com/index.php4.

In Alsace, and near Toulouse, there are labyrinths made from trimmed corn stalks that span twelve to thirty-five acres. Each year the mazes are completely remade and have different themes. Open May–August 10:30am to 7:30pm. Admission is 8.50 euros. Parc Enigmatis, Ferme de l'Hirondelle, Ribeauville; Tel: 03 89 41 80 81; Web site: www.labyrinthus.com.

The Merville Labyrinth is open until the end of September and is located twenty minutes northeast of Toulouse at Château de Merville. The Merville Labyrinth; Tel: 05 61 85 32 34; E-mail: merville@labyrinthus.fr.

In the southern most part of eastern France, the village of Vernet-les-Bains has been named a "center for green tourism." The village has made itself into a village-arboretum, filled with over 1,500 trees of two hundred varieties. The list of tree varieties can be found in French at www.villagearboretum.fr/liste.htm. The village has natural thermal springs and a health center specializing in respiratory and rheumatic ailments. Nearby, Canigou mountain in the eastern Pyrénées, which is considered sacred to French and Spanish Catalans, rises over nine thousand feet and has numerous hiking trails. Within a one- to two-hour walk from the village, you will find two abbeys, one of which is over one thousand years old and situated on a rocky outcropping. Five kilometers away is the walled city of Villefranche.

The Camargue, one of France's regional parks, is a protected nature reserve awaiting final designation as a World Heritage site by the United Nations. Located south of Arles, around Saintes-Maries-de-la-Mer, it comprises almost 250,000 acres of salt marshes and sand and salt dunes along the Mediterranean Sea. Natural sea salt from this area is sold in health food and gourmet food stores around the world (see more information under **Historical and Other Sites of Interest**). The Camargue includes extensive walking, biking, and horseback riding trails (see details under **Hiking**), as well as the Parc Ornithologique du Pont de Gau. For more information about the Camargue, go to www.parc-camargue.fr. At the bird sanctuary, Parc Ornithologique du Pont de Gau, four hundred species of birds have been sited, including herons, pink flamingos, storks, and sandpipers. Birds of prey can be observed in the raptor rehabilitation center. Binoculars are recommended, as well as natural bug repellent—the mosquitoes have a reputation for being prolific. Open seven days a week, 9am to sundown. Parc Ornithologique du Pont de Gau, les Sainte-Maries-de-la-Mer; www.parcornithologique.com.

Parc Ornithologique du Teich is a bird sanctuary located in the wetlands on the Bassin d'Arcachon. Le Teich is southwest of Bordeaux and east of Arcachon. You can train or bike the eight-and-a-half miles to Le Teich. The Le Teich train station is about a fifteen-minute walk from the sanctuary. Open July–August 10am to 8pm, September–June 10am to 6pm. Admission is 6.80 euros, and binoculars are available for rent at the ticket office. For more information, go to www.parc-ornithologique-du-teich.com/english/accueil.htm.

The Volerie des Aigles (Eagle Park) is located in the Alsace region of France in the Kintzheim Castle. La Volerie is a raptor sanctuary, as well as a rehabilitation and educational center, where you can see free-flying birds of prey. There is a shuttle bus from the Sélestat train station, which costs 4 euros for the day. Open April–November. La Volerie des Aigles, Château de Kintzheim, Kintzheim; Tel: 03 88 92 84 33; E-mail: promo@voleriedesaigles.com; Web site: www. voleriedesaigles.com/gb/.

La Montagne de Singes (Monkey Mountain) is a sixty-acre sanctuary and educational park in Kintzheim, not far from La Volerie des Aigles, with 280 free-roaming monkeys. The same shuttle bus serves Monkey Mountain and La Volerie. Open April–November. La Montagne de Singes; Tel: 03 88 92 11 09; E-mail: info@montagnedessinges.com; Web site: www.montagnedessinges.com.

La Forêt des Singes (The Forest of Monkeys) is a partner sanctuary with La Montagne de Singes, and it is located in southwestern France. La Forêt des Singes is a research center dedicated to examining the social life of the 130 free-roaming macaque monkeys. Located about ninety minutes from Toulouse and forty-five from Limoges, the center is in the town of Rocamadour, famous for its buildings and as a destination for religious pilgrims (see more details under Sacred

Regional Natural Parks in France

See www.parcs-naturels-regionaux.fr
for information on the all forty-five parks
throughout France

Sites). La Forêt des Singes, L'Hospitalet, Rocamadour; Tel: 05 65 33 6272; www.la-foret-des-singes.com.

For both birders and wildflower lovers, a trip to Mont Ventoux in Sault should not be missed. Recognized as a Biosphere Reserve by UNESCO in 1990, more than 120 bird species nest on Mt. Ventoux. It is also home to other wild animals, including hares, wild boar, foxes, deer, and a kind of wild sheep called Corsican mouflon. Le Mont Ventoux has more than four hundred species of flowers, including orchids, Greenland poppies, gentians, and Turk's-cap lilies. You will find more than one thousand plant varieties spread over five levels of vegetation, located between 400 and 1900 meters above sea level. See the *Green Earth Guide* Map to UNESCO Biosphere Reserves on page 124.

Fontaine-de-Vaucluse, the bluish-green source water of the Sorgue river, is sometimes nothing more than a water hole, but it can be impressive in the late winter and spring when it is full and gushing. It is located about four miles from Isle-sur-la-Sorgue in Provence.

The Luberon Park Visitors Center has a permanent exhibit about the history and geology of the Luberon. The Park covers over 400,000 acres and includes seventy towns. The Luberon mountain range runs sixty kilometers (about thirty-seven miles) east to west. For more information, go to www.parcduluberon.fr. There are 236 kilometers (145 miles) of cycling routes through the Luberon range, and routes are marked. For maps with routes, accommodations, and sites for the cyclist, go to www.veloloisirluberon.com.

Volunteer Tourism

If you want to work as a volunteer, there are two organizations that have ongoing projects in France. Search the following information and Web sites for current opportunities, and look under Europe-wide Information and Resources for more details about volunteering.

For opportunities to volunteer on organic farms, explore the World Wide Opportunities on Organic Farms (WWOOF), an international association with many participating farms in France. Farm choices can vary between large and small operations, and from vineyards to vegetables to goats. The France WWOOF is accessible through www.wwoof.fr. While the Web site is available in French or English, it is not fully functional at this time. If you find that is still true, please go to the international site at www.wwoof.org

Founded in 1982, Volunteers for Peace (VFP) is a nonprofit organization specializing in short-term (two to three weeks) volunteer opportunities around the world for people of all ages, and they have projects in France. Volunteers for Peace, 1034 Tiffany Road, Belmont, VT 05730-0202; Tel: 802-259-2759; E-mail: vfp@vfp.org; Web site: www.vfp.org.

Language Resources

The Deutsche Welle Radio Web site at www.dw-world.de offers free German language courses. The BBC Languages Web site offers free courses in French, Italian, Spanish, German, and other languages. For more information, go to www.bbc.co.uk/languages.

There are also a number of language podcast series available for free download, including tutorials in French, German, Italian, and Spanish.

Listed below are important phrases and words for traveling naturally, which are not usually found in conventional phrase books.

English	French	German	Italian	Spanish
herbs	herbe	Kraut/Krauter	erba	hierbas
herbalist	herboriste	Krauterheilkundife	erborista	yerbatero/ herboristeria
homeopathic	homeopathique	Homoopathisch	omeopatico	homeopatico
naturopathic doctor	le guerisseur-naturopathe	Heilpraktiker	il guaritore/ la guaritrice naturale	naturales medico
massage therapy	therapie de massage	Massagetherapie	terapia di massaggio	maseje
acupuncture	acuponcture	Akupunktur	agopuntura	acupuntura
TCM	medecine chinoise traditionnelle	Traditionelle chinesische medizin	medicina cinese tradizionale	la medicina tradicional china
drugstore/pharmacy	pharmacie	Apotheke/Drogerie/ Pharmacie	la pharmacia	farmacia
thrift store/ secondhand	Fripperie/fripe	brockenhaus	negozio di seconda mano	2a mano/ segunda mano
organic	biologique	biologishe	biologica	biologica

English	French	German	Italian	Spanish
street	rue	Strasse	via/strada	calle
train track	voie	Gleis	binari	via/vies

English	French	German	Italian	Spanish
please	s'il vous plait	Bitte (shon)	per favore	por favor
thank you	merci (beaucoup)	Danke (shon)	grazie	(muchas) gracias
excuse me	escusez-moi/pardon	Entschuldigung	mi scusi/perdono	perdóneme/excusa
you are welcome	je vous en prie	Bitte (shon)	prego	de nada

More Information about *Traveling Naturally*

We welcome your comments, suggestions, and insights. Please visit the *Traveling Naturally* Web site at www.travelingnaturally.com.

And visit the *Traveling Naturally* blog at travelingnaturally.blogspot. com for *Traveling Naturally* updates, and news about the upcoming *Green Earth Guide* to Spain, as well as other countries.

index

Bold page numbers indicate maps.

about the author

Dorian Yates has worked for consumer advocacy organizations as an environmental activist and congressional lobbyist; as an advisor on environmental, health, and social justice issues; and as a consultant on non-toxic products, indoor air quality, and  organic farming issues. A researcher and consultant for the books *The Green Pages* and *Ecopreneuring,* she lives in Vermont, United States.